TARENTINE HORSEMAN OF MAGNA GRAECIA

430–190 BC

NIC FIELDS   ILLUSTRATED BY SEÁN Ó'BRÓGÁIN

First published in Great Britain in 2008 by Osprey Publishing,
PO Box 883, Oxford, OX1 9PL, UK
PO Box 3985, New York, NY 10185-3985, USA
Email: info@ospreypublishing.com

Osprey Publishing is part of the Osprey Group.

Transferred to digital print on demand 2015.

First published 2008
1st impression 2008

Printed and bound in Great Britain.

A CIP catalogue record for this book is available from the British Library.

ISBN: 978 1 84603 279 0

Page layout by Scribe, Oxford, UK
Index by Alan Thatcher
Typeset in Sabon and Myriad Pro
Map by Trevor Bounford
Originated by PPS Grasmere, Leeds, UK

Artist's note

Readers may care to note that the original paintings from which the colour plates in this book were prepared are available for private sale. All reproduction copyright whatsoever is retained by the Publishers. All enquiries should be addressed to:

Seán Ó'Brógáin
Stragally
Commeen (R253)
Cloghan
Lifford
Donegal
Ireland

The Publishers regret that they can enter into no correspondence upon this matter.

Editor's note

The following abbreviations have been used throughout the text to refer to source material:

Fornara	C.W. Fornara, *Translated Documents of Greece and Rome I: Archaic Times to the end of the Peloponnesian War 2* (Cambridge, 1983)
Harding	P. Harding, *Translated Documents of Greece and Rome 2: From the end of the Peloponnesian War to the battle of Ipsus* (Cambridge, 1985)
IG	*Inscriptiones Graecae* (Berlin, 1923)
Vlasto	O.E. Ravel, *Descriptive Catalogue of the Collection of Tarentine Coins formed by M.P. Vlasto* (London, 1947)

The Woodland Trust

Osprey Publishing is supporting the Woodland Trust, the UK's leading woodland conservation charity, by funding the dedication of trees.

www.ospreypublishing.com

CONTENTS

TARENTINE HORSEMAN OF MAGNA GRAECIA

430 BC–190 BC

The Spartan settlers of Taras chose as the site of their urban centre the tip of a slender promontory, which was thus provided with natural defences. In this area have been found the remains of an early sixth-century Doric temple, seen here in Piazza Castello. (Fields-Carré Collection)

INTRODUCTION

According to historical tradition, Taras, on the instep of Italy and now known as Taranto, was founded in 706 BC, and archaeological evidence indicates that such a date cannot be far wrong. The earliest and simplest reason for its foundation is given by Aristotle as an instance of the divisions that may arise in a state when the aristocracy assigns to itself all the political privileges, "for example the so-called Partheniai, whom the Spartans detected in a conspiracy and sent away to be the founders of Taras" (*Politics* 1306b27).

The name Partheniai is not adequately explained by Aristotle. In other authors it is constantly associated with the word *parthenos*, virgin, and the most straightforward explanation is that is a term of contempt used by one political faction of their erstwhile opponents. According to a contemporary of Aristotle, Ephoros of Kyme (in a passage quoted by Strabo), the Partheniai were the sons of unmarried mothers born during the First Messenian War (*c.* 730–710 BC). As the war turned out to be a lengthy conflict, Spartan women left at home for the duration reportedly wanted to avoid the risk of a future shortage of men. Hence they sent a delegation to their husbands to point out that they were fighting on unequal terms, that is, the Messenians were staying at home and fathering children while the Spartans had left their wives virtually as widows. The men had sworn not to return until victorious, but yielded to the arguments of their women and sent home from the army some youngsters with orders to bed all the virgin girls of Sparta. However, when the Spartan warriors at long last won the war and marched home, they repudiated the offspring of these illicit unions and denied them the rights accorded to other citizens because of their illegitimacy. Their subordinate status provoked them into rebellion, which was successfully put down.

It was decided to send Phalanthos, the leader of the dissidents, to consult Apollo's oracle at Delphi, who gave the following response: "I give you Satyrion, both to settle

the rich land of Taras and to be the scourge of the Iapygii" (Strabo 6.3.2). The oracle's message, probably *post eventum*, thus defines the focal points of the territory of the colony: the urban centre and its eastern outpost, and anticipates the struggle against the indigenous population, the Iapygii, that Taras would have to face throughout its history. The Greek name Satyrion has been preserved in the modern one of Porto Saturo, 12km (7.5 miles) to the east of Taranto, indicating the former Greek character of this corner of Italy. The site, before the foundation of the colony, was occupied by a large native community that was destroyed by the Greeks, who replaced it with their own settlement, as is confirmed by the existence of a necropolis that was already receiving customers in the seventh century BC.

The urban centre itself was established in an exceptionally fine location, on a slender promontory stretching from east to west between an outer bay (today known as Mare Grande) and an inner lagoon (Mare Piccolo). Between the western extremity and the mainland opposite was a channel, which ran north into the lagoon. This magnificent body of water was some 26km (16 miles) in circumference and provided the best harbour in southern Italy. The urban centre of Taras was thus surrounded by water on three sides: the circular lagoon in the north, by the narrow sound in the west, and by the deep bay and open sea to the south. It was understandably small, covering an area of about 16ha (40 acres), but between it and its eastern outpost lay good arable lands. As well as Satyrion, an extensive network of farming villages occupied the coastal plain around Taras.

One possible way for us to rationalise the mythical foundation story is to view the so-called illegitimate founders of Taras as colonists disgruntled at not receiving their fair share of the conquered land in Messenia, the south-western quarter of the Peloponnese, following the success of the Spartans in the First Messenian War. In the Greek world, after all, the ownership of land was the essential qualification for the acquisition of political rights. So excluded from the sharing-out of the spoils of a long and difficult war, this group of Spartans are forced to colonise overseas. Whatever the reasons behind all this, it is clear they were considered an inferior group within the ruling body.

View looking north across modern Sparta (founded 1834). The slight, wooded rise on the edge of the modern city, seen here in the middle background, once served as the acropolis of the ancient city. Taras was the Spartans' only genuine overseas colonial foundation. (Fields-Carré Collection)

Though we choose not to believe the embellishments that surround the foundation story, in a sense Taras was the bastard child of its stern parent, Sparta. For more than two centuries the Tarentines lived under a monarchy and had no close political connections with Sparta. The last is hardly surprising considering the alleged reasons for their departure in the first place. Yet despite their complete political autonomy, the Tarentines, like the Spartans, were Dorians in the fullest sense – speaking a Doric dialect of Greek, preserving Dorian social and political institutions, and worshipping the god who of all the Olympians was most closely associated with the Dorian peoples, namely Apollo. The colonists, as colonists tended to do, reproduced their mother city both in the composition of the citizens and in the social structures and methods of political organisation at the time of the foundation.

Unlike Sparta, however, Taras came to boast a class of horsemen who excelled in valour and could provide their own horse and equipment from the wealthiest citizens of the city-state. Xenophon (b. *c.* 428 BC), the Athenian-born soldier-of-fortune and essayist, whose profound interest in cavalry and his

knowledge of its use are apparent in his treatises on commanding cavalry and horsemanship, contends with some force that Spartan horsemen were diabolical, since the wealthiest Spartans reared the horses but the riders only appeared when war was declared. Worse still, as Xenophon bemoans, "the men who served in the cavalry were the ones who were in the worse physical condition and the least anxious to win distinction" (*Hellenika* 6.4.11). The quality of the horses and the efficiency of the riders can only be imagined. In Sparta, which could boast of being the birthplace of Leonidas and the Three Hundred, and which was justly famed for its armoured spearmen, no self-respecting citizen would be expected to fight on horseback. Thucydides (b. *c.* 455 BC) reports that the Spartans only established a force of 400 horsemen in 424 BC because it was the only effective way of countering Athenian hit-and-run raids, emphasising that this step was "quite at variance with their normal way of doing things" (4.55.2). However, Taras, with the good river-lands of Apulia (modern-day Puglia) at its disposal, was the

Tarentine silver didrachma (Period VIII, Vlasto 937) with two young horsemen. Taras continued Spartan traditions, and these are Helen's brothers – the Dioskouroi. The pride of Sparta, Castor was famous as a tamer of horses, Polydeuces as the best boxer of his day. (Fondazione E. Pomarici-Santomasi/Franco Taccogna)

Magna Graecia

Beginning in the eighth century BC, various communities from mainland Greece and the Aegean began to plant colonies along the Italian seaboard. The earliest, at Pithekoussai (Ischia), an island off the Bay of Naples, was initially founded by Greeks from Euboia (Evvía) as a trading station and a staging post for Greek entrepreneurs on the coastal voyage north up the shin of Italy to Etruria. But from the late eighth century BC other Greek settlements were founded on the fertile coastal plains of southern Italy and Sicily so as to relieve population pressures back home, and to become sources of grain and other supplies for the mother cities. However, unlike colonies in the modern sense of that word, they were totally independent foundations and not subject to their mother cities, though they normally retained close cultural and sentimental links.

Scholars have yet to agree on the origins of the general term Greater Greece or Magna Graecia (*Megále Hellás* in Greek), nor are they certain when it was first coined. Its first mention seems to be by Polybios, the Greek soldier-historian living in Rome in the second century BC, who ascribes the term to Pythagoras (b. *c.* 570 BC) and his great philosophical school at Kroton. In the age of Augustus, the geographer Strabo associates the term with the territory conquered by the colonists from Greece. Modern commentators have their own explanations. Some feel the term refers to the Greek influence in Italy, which goes back at least as early as the sixth century BC, while others think it was the Romans who coined the term, comparing this region, in a strictly geographic sense, with the Greek mainland, which in their view was rather restricted because of its mountainous nature. The debate has yet to be resolved. However, we are reasonably certain about the boundaries of this territory, which in Roman times meant all that part of southern Italy, except for Sicily, taken over by Greek colonisation. For sake of argument, in this publication, Magna Graecia will refer to the widely scattered Greek communities of southern Italy, of which there were approximately twenty.

breeding-ground for large numbers of warhorses. Strabo (6.3.9), although writing in the Augustan era, indicated that much of Apulia, especially the heel of Italy, was suitable for the rearing of horses and had supplied cavalry mounts both for the Tarentines and the Iapygii with whom they warred. Little wonder then, that with Apulia celebrated throughout antiquity for its fine horseflesh, the Greek colonists would come to exploit this natural advantage.

THE ORIGINS OF THE HORSEMEN OF TARAS

The origins of the horsemen of Taras go back to the fifth century BC. From its foundation until then Taras remained small and only moderately wealthy, engaging from time to time in border wars with the locals and in rivalry with the other Greeks of southern Italy, which was so densely colonised that it became known as Magna Graecia (see commentary on page 7). In some of these quarrels Taras was successful, and the Tarentines marked their victories by dedicating offerings to Apollo at Delphi. But at the hands of their inveterate enemies the Iapygii, in 473 BC or thereabouts they suffered a thundering defeat that destroyed much of their citizen militia. The events were chronicled by Herodotos (b. c. 484 BC), who defines it as "the worst slaughter of Greeks... the losses of the Tarentines were

too many to count" (7.170.3). We learn from Aristotle that this disaster, involving the flower of Tarentine aristocracy, was the catalyst for the overthrow of the ruling élite "the government was turned into a democracy" (*Politics* 1303a3) and, we can safely assume, a radical shake-up of the Tarentine army or what was left of it.

From the second half of the fifth century BC onwards Taras had a fairly effective democratic constitution, which provided internal stability, while externally it began its rise to the pre-eminent place among the Greek cities of Magna Graecia, which it was to enjoy for close on two centuries. The rapid recovery of Taras and the subsequent attempts to establish a mini-empire in its own backyard was a direct consequence of the reconstruction of its citizen militia, of which the horsemen were a necessary, or even indispensable, part. Strabo estimates that in its halcyon days during the mid-fourth century BC, Taras could mobilise 30,000 infantry, 3,000 cavalry and "one thousand *hipparchoi*" (6.3.4), but this was probably paper strength. The Greek term *hipparchos* usually refers to a cavalry commander, but the plural form here, if indeed Strabo is correct, probably denotes the citizen horsemen themselves.

Profiting from the growing weakness of its nearest rivals within Magna Graecia, Metapontion and Kroton, Taras turned its own expansionist aims westward, engaging in war with Thourioi (present-day Sibari), a colony recently founded with Athenian help and participation. The contest ended around 433 BC with the establishment of the colony of Herakleia under the control of Taras. The victorious citizens honoured the chief of the Olympian gods, for a bronze butt-spike (which not only acted as a counterweight but also as a spare point in the event that the spearhead should be broken off) has been subsequently discovered at Olympia bearing the inscription: "Spoils from the Thourians the Tarentines dedicated to Zeus Olympios as a tithe" (Fornara 112). Of course, as well as the religion of the old world, there was its politics too. When Athens sent an armada to Sicily in 415 BC, Taras took the side of Dorian city-state of Syracuse and that of the mother city, Sparta, while a local chieftain, called Artas in the Greek tongue, supplied the Athenians with Iapygian javelineers.

In the course of the fifth century BC the urban centre underwent a radical change that modified the layout of Taras. An expansion took place beyond its original confines onto the mainland to the east. Laid out in rectangular fashion, with straight streets crossing at right angles, this urban redevelopment was buttressed by a circuit wall some 11km (6.9 miles) long. The fortifications incorporated elaborate gateways, towers and other defensive features such as an outer ditch, and enclosed an area of 530ha (1,360 acres). This massive increase in urban space doubtless corresponded with the democratic reformation of Taras. A series of reforms would have removed political privilege from the aristocratic élite of the city, which meant an extension of political rights with a consequent enlargement of the body politic.

At the same time Taras vigorously asserted its economic independence by minting its own silver coinage, something that Sparta never found necessary to do. Coinage began here sometime around 500 BC, and characteristic of Tarentine issues of coins was the horsemen series of legends, which first appear in the last quarter of the fifth century BC, bearing the

Marble bust (Naples, Museo Archeologico Nazionale, 6156) of Archidamos III, son of Agesilaos and king of Sparta. This is a Roman copy of a portrait statue of the king set up at Olympia not long after he fought and died as a mercenary on behalf of Taras. (Fields-Carré Collection)

devices of *ephors* or *stratêgoi*. The elected magistrates, *ephors*, were clearly adopted from Sparta, while the latter office was known during the life of Archytas, the native Tarentine who was a Pythagorean philosopher, mathematician, and close associate of Plato. The post of *stratêgos*, the highest civic magistracy of democratic Taras, was obviously unknown in monarchical Sparta and therefore Taras did not remain entirely faithful to the metropolitan model of the mother city. Archytas himself was elected *stratêgos* with full powers for seven consecutive years, from 367 BC to 361 BC. Although the exact details of his career are lacking, the Archytas period of political dominance coincides with the height of Tarentine power in Magna Graecia. In military terms, the horsemen of Taras were noted for their prowess during this period, and Archytas' victories are an indication of the efficiency of the citizen militia. Following the untimely death of Archytas, close to 350 BC, the delicate political balance that the philosopher had succeeded in creating crumbled.

Yet the horseman was to remain the device of Taras for at least another century and a quarter, a testimony to Tarentine interest in horses and horsemanship. Another notable feature of Tarentine coinage, especially in the post-Archytas era, is the number and frequency of gold issues. These can often be associated with one or other of the succession of Greek warlords invited by the Tarentines to help them in their wars in return for payment.

Confronting the barbarians: Taras at war

After the death of Archytas Taras' reputation for martial greatness, achieved in no small part by the prowess of its horsemen, suffered. The warlike qualities of its citizen body took an appreciable nosedive, and the talented general

HORSEMAN OF TARAS

This citizen-trooper, from the time of the war with Thourioi, wears the high soft-leather boots now popular with Greek horsemen. Xenophon (*Peri Hippikes* 12.10) recommends this type of footwear for the aspiring horseman as they protected both his shins and feet. Also much favoured was the *petasos*, a broad-brimmed hat of yellowish-tan felt, which offered protection against the sun and dust rather than against the enemy. He also wears a short tunic, the *chitôn*, girded at the waist and pinned at the shoulder, and over this garment a short cloak, the *chlamys*, but no body armour. At this date Greek horsemen in general wore little or no armour and did not carry shields.

Our horseman's whole outfit was in no sense a uniform as hunters, shepherds, travellers, or anybody else whose occupation called him to vigorous outdoor activity commonly wore it. If by no other article of dress, the horseman might be definitely distinguished by his spurs. The Greeks used a simple prick spur, with a short but sharp point, fastened either to the bare heel or, as here, to the boot. Spurs were usually made of bronze.

In battle the horseman relied upon the javelin as an offensive weapon. It differed from the spear in that it was lighter and was thrown rather than thrust. It enabled a man to attack the enemy from a distance, and was particularly effective when thrown from horseback. Xenophon recommends the Persian *paltà* of tough cornel wood, for "the skilful man may throw the one and can use the other in front or on either side or behind" (*Peri Hippikes* 12.12). Approximately 1.8m long and about the diameter of a human thumb, Persian javelins were shorter and stronger than the Greek spear. Of course, we should remember that Xenophon had spent much time in the company of the Persians, hence his willingness to adopt foreign weapons.

Pyrrhos (318–272 BC) himself was to find the Tarentines lazy, luxurious and loath to fight. Increasingly unable to adequately defend themselves against the indigenous peoples that continued to threaten them, the Tarentines had first appealed to their warlike mother city for help. In 343 BC Sparta sent one of its two joint kings, Archidamos, with an army composed of fellow Spartans and Greek mercenaries. For five years or so he enjoyed some success against the Iapygii before he was struck down in a skirmish.

Soon afterwards, when Alexander the Great was busy overrunning the east, Alexander of Molossia, who was both his uncle and brother-in-law, gladly accepted another Tarentine invitation to intervene in Magna Graecia. Arriving in 334 BC, he quickly proved to be an effective general, with a run of victories against the Iapygii and Oscans (there is evidence that his venture had his brother-in-law's approval, if not his active backing). Three years on and he too was to fall in a casual brush with the locals.

A third and fourth episode of this kind involved the two sons of Kleomenes, king of Sparta. The eldest, Akrotatos, arrived in 314 BC, but his boorish and brutal behaviour antagonised his employers and he had to return to Sparta under a cloud. Akrotatos' younger brother, Kleonymos, too, fought for Taras as a mercenary. He landed in 303 BC with an expeditionary force of some 5,000 mercenaries, recruited a further 5,000 troops in Italy, and began to carve out a pocket kingdom for himself. Though his main focus was Magna Graecia, where he campaigned successfully against the Oscans, Kleonymos also operated across the Adriatic in Corcyra (modern-day Corfu), an island of obvious strategic value on the straits between Italy and Greece. However, like his brother before him, he too eventually fell out with his employers, and Kleonymos departed, with some rancour, in 301 BC.

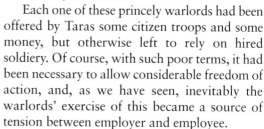

Each one of these princely warlords had been offered by Taras some citizen troops and some money, but otherwise left to rely on hired soldiery. Of course, with such poor terms, it had been necessary to allow considerable freedom of action, and, as we have seen, inevitably the warlords' exercise of this became a source of tension between employer and employee.

Rome too did not hesitate to become involved in the fighting, accepting a request from distant Thourioi for help against the incursions of the Oscans. Rome sent a small fleet, but previously, when the Romans had not been particularly interested in Apulia or the south, a treaty had been drawn up between Rome and Taras by which it was agreed that Roman warships would not cruise eastwards beyond the Lacinian promontory (Cape Colonne) 12km south of Kroton. Ten Roman ships did so; and as a result, four were sunk, another captured and the rest scattered by the Tarentine navy. They followed up this success on the high seas by marching to Thourioi, driving out the Roman garrison and replacing its oligarchic government with a democratic one. Rome sent envoys to demand satisfaction, but on arrival in Taras they were mocked before an assembly in the city's theatre, or so it was claimed. One citizen was even said to have thrown excrement at one envoy and to have made fun of his barbaric Latin, upon which Rome declared war in 281 BC.

The Greek historian Polybius, who wrote a narrative history of Roman expansion in this period, had no doubts that the Romans of his own and earlier times wanted to grow from a village by the Tiber to a world empire. After the conquest of the Latins, they went on to defeat the Etruscans, Gauls, and Samnites, and so when the Tarentines invited the intervention of Pyrrhos, Polybios continues, "they now for the first time made war upon the rest of Italy, not as if its inhabitants were foreigners, but as if the country were already rightfully theirs" (1.6.6).

In any case, in Roman eyes, the Greeks were no good at war. Taras had maintained its ground in Magna Graecia by hiring professional soldiers from Greece, and so decided to hire another foreign army. There was one ready to hand, under Pyrrhos, warrior-king of Epeiros, who wanted nothing better than to unite all the Greeks of Magna Graecia and Sicily under his rule. He accepted the Tarentine contract and crossed the Adriatic and confronted the Romans for the first time with professional troops who had been trained in the world-conquering tactics of his cousin, Alexander the Great. He also brought another Hellenistic novelty: twenty war elephants.

Attic stele (Eleusis, Museum of Archaeology, 5101) from the period of the great war between Athens and Sparta (431–404 BC), depicting a fight between Athenian horsemen and Spartan hoplites. Sparta was justly famed for its hoplites, but not so for its horsemen. (Fields-Carré Collection)

His first bloody victory over Roman troops was near the Tarentine colony of Herakleia in 280 BC, after which he dashed northwards to Rome and sent his trusted envoy, Kineas, to offer terms to the Senate. Kineas offered to restore all prisoners and to end the war, if the Romans would make peace with Taras, grant autonomy to the Greeks, and return all territory conquered from the Oscans. He was bluntly refused, and he was said to have reported to his king that Rome was like a many-headed monster whose armies would keep on being replenished. If this was true, then Kineas was a shrewd judge of Roman manpower.

After this refusal Pyrrhos won a second bloody victory at Asculum in 279 BC, a bruising two-day engagement in which his elephants played a major role. Once again, the casualties on both sides were heavy. "Another such victory", Pyrrhos is said to have remarked, "and we shall be lost" (Plutarch *Pyrrhos* 21.9) – whence our saying of a "Pyrrhic victory" for any success bought at too high a price.

In 278 BC Pyrrhos faced a choice: either to turn back to Macedon where recent events gave him a chance of gaining the throne, or else to turn to Sicily, in keeping with his former marriage to a Syracusan princess. While continuing to protect Taras, he chose to go south to Sicily where he now promised freedom from the Carthaginians, who had high hopes of occupying the entire island. For three years he showed no more commitment to real freedom than any true Hellenistic prince and failed in his hopes. The plans of Carthage were indeed thwarted, but the swashbuckling Pyrrhos overstayed his welcome in war-weary Sicily. On his return journey to Italy he lost several of his elephants when he was attacked by the Carthaginian fleet, and he failed to win the crucial encounter against the Romans at Malventum in 275 BC, soon to be renamed Beneventum. So Pyrrhos sailed back across the Adriatic. As for Taras, well the days of a free Magna Graecia were doomed. In 272 BC the Romans took control of troublesome Taras, allowing the garrison that Pyrrhos had left there to withdraw on honourable terms.

THE ROLE OF THE HORSEMEN OF TARAS

Our story now shifts back slightly to the time when the triumphs of Alexander the Great had given way to infighting among his generals and other rival claimants to his vast legacy. His fantastic conquests had made the language and culture of the Greeks dominant throughout much of the east, but his death in 323 BC ushered in a period of perpetual warfare among his successors – Antigonos Monophthalmos, Eumenes of Kardia, Kassandros, Ptolemy, Lysimachos, and Seleukos – as they jockeyed for power. It was a time for grim warlords and their private armies.

Marble bust (Selçuk, Arkeoloji Müzesi, 1846) of Lysimachos. Made satrap of Thrace, he joined the coalition against Antigonos (316 BC) and eventually assumed the title of king (306 BC). Taking Macedon and Thessaly from Demetrios (288 BC), aged eighty, he was to fall in battle fighting Seleukos. (Fields-Carré Collection)

It was a time too for the horsemen known specifically as Tarentines to make their first appearance on the stage of history. This occurred in 317 BC when 2,200 horsemen under the command of Peithon of Media, "who had come up with him from the sea", explains Diodoros, "men selected for their skill in ambushes and their loyalty" (19.29.2), fought for the one-eyed Antigonos on his left wing at Paraitakene (near present-day Isfahan, Iran). Another hundred Tarentines formed a screen forward of the right, his offensive wing. Early in the following year, force-marching to the district of Gabiene near Sousa, 200 of these Tarentines formed part of Antigonos' advance guard (Diodoros 19.39.2).

Some four years later the Tarentines reappear, on this particular occasion fighting at Gaza for Antigonos' flamboyant, impetuous son Demetrios (the Taker of Cities, *Poliorketes*, as he was later called) in his first role as an independent commander. Around a hundred strong, they were organised into three tactical units, known as *ilai*, and formed an advanced guard forward of the left, the offensive wing of his army (Diodoros 19.82.2). They frequently occur thereafter, not only in the armies of the Hellenistic east, but those of old Greece too, albeit in small numbers, although some doubts have been raised as to whether their provenance was always Taras itself. Indeed, in some of the smaller instances, the term Tarentine may have been used to refer to groups of mercenary cavalry who operated in the same fashion as the original horsemen of Taras.

With the gradual decay of the short-term citizen militia of the Greek world, small forces of trained professionals became more and more common. For instance, when Pyrrhos swept into Taras he immediately took charge of affairs by placing the whole city on a war footing. According to Plutarch, all places of entertainment and sport were closed, all festivities and social events were postponed and the population conscripted for military service. Some of the

Campanian painted dish (Rome, Museo Nazionale di Villa Giulia), war elephant and calf. Unmistakably an Indian elephant (*Elephas indicus*), and possibly one of those brought by Pyrrhos. Florus describes (1.13.12) how a cow-elephant, anxious for her offspring's safety, spread havoc among Pyrrhos' troops. (Fields-Carré Collection)

citizens, who objected very strongly to this treatment, left town. As Plutarch says, "they were so unaccustomed to discipline that they regarded it as a slavery not to be allowed to live as they pleased" (*Pyrrhos* 16.7).

Taras may have become a byword for opulence and luxurious living but there was still a branch of its citizens who could provide an effective fighting force, namely its horsemen, who could either be deployed for home defence or offered for hire overseas. A number of Athenian stone inscriptions survive, which refer to horsemen known as *Tarantinoi*, who had been in the service of this state. Thus we know of the existence in the second century BC of a torch race on horseback for the Tarentines as one of the events in the Theseian games, a local contest for teams assembled from the ten tribes of Athens (*IG* 2^2 958.56–61, 960.33, 961.34). Perhaps this was an equestrian event copied from mercenaries stationed in Athens at an earlier date, either those in the pay

Nereid monument (London, British Museum, 885), hoplite and horseman. The tomb (c. 390–380 BC) from which this slab came is at Xanthós in Lycia. It belonged to a local dynast who, like his master the Persian king, employed Greek mercenaries to stiffen native levies. (Fields-Carré Collection)

of Demetrios or of the state itself. Polyainos (3.7.1, 4) certainly mentions Tarentines in connection with one of his two sieges of the city (307 BC, 297–295 BC), and likewise he places Tarentines in Athens during the tyranny of Lachares (300–295 BC). There exists also an inscription (*IG* 2² 2975) that records a dedication of spoils by them, though which enemy and what war history has not recorded. In all probability the inscription was made at the turn of the third century BC, that is to say, at the time of the new tyranny. From this period we also have an inscription (Agora I 7587), set up by a contingent of Tarentines in 280 BC, honouring the Athenian cavalry officers of the previous year under whom they served.

Some 85 years earlier Xenophon had advised his fellow citizens to recruit 200 mercenaries so as to bring their cavalry corps up to establishment and enhance its fighting capabilities. Strangely, by way of example, he cited the Spartan cavalry, which he claimed first gained its reputation with the incorporation of "foreign horsemen" (*Hipparchikos* 9.4). In fact, Xenophon was talking as an eyewitness, as he was clearly referring to the highly effective mounted arm created by Agesilaos in Anatolia (*Hellenika* 3.4.15) and not the native horsemen of Sparta that he disparages at the time of the catastrophic Leuktra campaign (*Hellenika* 6.4.10–11, 13). It seems that the Athenians, with their employment of Tarentines, had at last heeded the advice of Xenophon, who, after all, was the leading expert on equestrian matters.

For the best part of fifty years the Tarentines fade out of history, which is hardly surprising when we consider the sources for that period as a whole are very scarce. Be that as it may, wherever their whereabouts during that time, the Tarentines unexpectedly re-enter our story in Sparta. The Spartans had once been the most feared warriors in Greece, but by the second half of the third century BC society in Sparta was in many ways much like that of other Greek states; to play even in the second division of Hellenistic warfare, mercenaries had become almost a necessity. And so, in the campaigning season of 226 BC, a contingent of Tarentines is found fighting on behalf of the Spartan king Kleomenes near Megalopolis in the central Peloponnese (Plutarch *Kleomenes* 6.3). Again in the central Peloponnese, at the battle of Mantineia (207 BC), Tarentines fought for Machanidas of Sparta. As they also fought for the opposition that day, namely Philopoimen of the Achaian League, the Tarentines on both sides were without doubt mercenaries (Polybios 11.12.6, Polyainos 3.7.1). As the leading soldier and statesman in the Achaian League, which included Achaia proper and much of Arcadia along with Corinth, Argos and Sikyon, Philopoimen saw fit to transform the cavalry of the coalition forces from a worthless body into an impressive fighting arm. The corps was clearly aristocratic and wealthy as Plutarch describes its members as "the most esteemed of the citizens" (*Philopoimen* 18.4), and in all his campaigns Philopoimen led an Achaian levy stiffened by a good number of mercenaries including, of course, Tarentines.

The finale of Mantineia was fairly Homeric in style, the two leaders meeting in single combat on horseback, Philopoimen striking the mortal blow with his spear, then reversing it to stab Machanidas with the butt-spike. The dead king was replaced by the far tougher Nabis (r. 207–192 BC), who adopted the very un-Spartan trappings of Hellenistic monarchy, such as keeping a personal bodyguard of mercenaries and putting his image on coins. Despite the growing threat of Rome, Sparta and Achaia remained divided both by ideology and a hatred that stemmed from repeated attempts by the League to incorporate Sparta. After the death of Nabis, Sparta was finally forced into the Achaian League, thus ending its independent history. Its walls were razed and, in the words of Livy, a proclamation issued stating "that all foreign mercenaries who had served under the tyrants should quit Spartan territory" (38.34.1). As a result, all Tarentine horsemen currently in service were required to return home.

In the aftermath of Hannibal's defeat in 202 BC, the Romans turned their attention towards the east. Ostensibly in response to appeals from Pergamon and Rhodes, Rome decided to intervene in Greece before Philip V of Macedon (r. 221–179 BC) and Antiochos III of Syria (r. 223–187 BC) had a chance to upset the balance of power in the east.

Tarentine silver didrachma (Period VII, Vlasto 804–7), youth on horseback and an inscription scratched on an Ionic capital. The term 'Tarentine' now denoted a type of horseman rather than a nationality, and thus only referred to weaponry and tactics. (Fondazione E. Pomarici-Santomasi/ Franco Taccogna)

Marble bust of Xenophon (Bergama, Arkeoloji Müzesi, 784). Born into a well-to-do Athenian family, as a youth he served in the Athenian cavalry corps before turning his hand to professional soldiering. First serving the younger Kyros, he later fought for Sparta under King Agesilaos. (Fields-Carré Collection)

One of the greatest Hellenistic monarchs who, in conscious imitation of Alexander, bore the epithet 'the Great', Antiochos attempted to re-constitute the Syrian kingdom by bringing back into the fold the former outlying possessions. He thus managed to re-assert Seleukid power briefly in the upper satrapies and Anatolia, but then foolishly challenged Rome for control of Greece in 194 BC. Towards the end of 190 BC Rome, backed by Pergamon and Rhodes, won the final battle over Antiochos on the level plain of Magnesia in Lydia, driving that magnificent and ambitious king back across the Taurus. On that fateful day Antiochos had Tarentines on the left wing of his army (Livy 37.40, Polybios 20.3.7), and, as far as we know, this seems to be their last appearance on the stage of history. Polybios, whom Livy drew upon for his account of the battle, records some 500 Tarentines being employed by Antiochos ten years earlier in 200 BC, but in his detailed description of the Seleukid military parade staged at Daphne (166 BC) they are conspicuous by their absence (30.25.3–11). But as Polybios himself earlier reports, by the treaty of Apameia (188 BC) the kings of Syria had been forbidden "to recruit mercenaries from the territory subject to Rome" (21.43.10). They were thus cut off from the recruiting grounds such as old Greece and Magna Graecia. As the dominance of Rome grew, the role of Tarentine horsemen, and other independent mercenary groups, invariably declined.

CHRONOLOGY

The following dates refer to key events in the history of Taras, as well as important dates within the wider Mediterranean world.

c. 730–710 BC	First Messenian War.
c. 706 BC	Foundation of Taras.
c. 473 BC	Destruction of Tarentine army by Iapygii.
443 BC	Foundation of Thourioi.
433 BC	Foundation of Herakleia.
431–404 BC	Peloponnesian War fought between Athens and its empire and the Peloponnesian League led by Sparta.
c. 428 BC	Birth of Xenophon.
415 BC	Athenian expedition to Sicily.
413 BC	Destruction of Athenian expedition.
405 BC	Dionysios takes power in Syracuse.
404 BC	Athens surrenders to Sparta.
387 BC	Plato visits court of Dionysios.
371 BC	Spartans defeated at Leuktra.
367–361 BC	Archytas becomes *stratêgos* of Taras.
356 BC	Dion liberates Syracuse.
c. 350 BC	Death of Archytas.
341 BC	Archidamos III hired by Taras.
338 BC	Archidamos killed. Philip II of Macedon defeats the Greeks at Chaironeia.

336 BC	Assassination of Philip II.
334 BC	Alexander of Molossia hired by Taras. Alexander the Great crosses the Granikos river.
331 BC	Alexander of Molossia killed. Alexander the Great victorious at Gaugamela.
323 BC	Death of Alexander the Great in Babylon. Start of the War of the Successors – the struggle for supremacy amongst Alexander's former generals.
317 BC	Antigonos defeats Eumenes at Paraitakene.
316 BC	Antigonos defeats Eumenes at Gabiene and he is executed. Agathokles takes power in Syracuse.
314 BC	Akrotatos hired by Taras.
312 BC	Ptolemy and Seleukos defeat Demetrios at Gaza.
307 BC	Demetrios takes Athens from Kassandros.
307–304 BC	Kassandros besieges Athens.
306 BC	Demetrios defeats Ptolemy at Salamis.
305–304 BC	Demetrios besieges Rhodes.
304 BC	Demetrios lifts siege of Athens.
303 BC	Kleonymos hired by Taras.
301 BC	Antigonos defeated and killed at Ipsos. Athens gains freedom. Kleonymos dismissed.
300–295 BC	Lachares becomes tyrant of Athens.
297–295 BC	Demetrios besieges Athens.
294 BC	Demetrios seizes Macedon.
287 BC	Athens revolts from Demetrios.
286 BC	Demetrios captured by Seleukos.
283 BC	Death of Demetrios.
281 BC	Rome declares war on Taras. Pyrrhos of Epeiros hired by Taras
280 BC	Pyrrhos defeats the Romans at Herakleia.
279 BC	Pyrrhos defeats the Romans at Asculum.
278 BC	Pyrrhos sails to Sicily.
275 BC	Romans defeat Pyrrhos at Malventum.
272 BC	Romans take Taras. Pyrrhos killed at Argos.

ABOVE
Tarentine silver didrachma (Period VI, Vlasto 673) with a youth crowning his horse. Unlike its monarchical mother city, democratic Taras established a useful cavalry arm. With the fertile lands of Apulia to hand, conditions were right for the raising of horses. (Fondazione E. Pomarici-Santomasi/ Franco Taccogna)

243 BC	Aratos captures Acrocorinth.
226 BC	Kleomenes III defeats Achaian League near Megalopolis.
218 BC	Hannibal crosses Alps.
217 BC	Antiochos III defeated at Raphia.
215 BC	Alliance of Philip V of Macedon and Hannibal.
207 BC	Philopoimen defeats and kills Machanidas at Mantineia.
197 BC	Romans defeat Philip V at Kynoskephalai.
196 BC	Romans proclaim Greek freedom.
192 BC	Assassination of Nabis.
190 BC	Romans defeat Antiochos at Magnesia.

RECRUITMENT

In terms of the use of cavalry, the Greek colonies of Magna Graecia and Sicily were well in advance of the motherland. However, Taras only instituted a proper cavalry corps after the establishment of democracy, its members being recruited from those wealthy enough to own and maintain a horse. As such, by the mid-fifth century BC there was a body of 1,000 aristocratic horsemen.

As in later armies, the horsemen of Taras formed an élite corps within the army. For most of its history, it was decidedly aristocratic in composition and represented only a tiny proportion of the fighting forces of Taras. Such a powerful aristocratic formation may seem a paradox in a democracy, but owning a horse was very costly. Aristotle remarks that "horse-breeding requires the ownership of large resources" (*Politics* 1321a11), while Xenophon not only confirms this need for "ample means" but also stresses that horse-breeders should also have an interest in "affairs of state and of war" (*Peri Hippikes* 2.1). As one of the most prominent symbols of wealth and prestige was the breeding or owning of horses, the cavalry of democratic Taras served as one of the last bastions of its aristocratic rich.

Sculpture and vase painting present the view that the horsemen of Taras were young. So as well as wealthy and aristocratic, the cavalry corps was an essentially youthful organisation. For young men, it seems, had the skill, strength and stamina to ride on horseback without stirrups and saddle in sometimes difficult equestrian manoeuvres on uneven and hazardous terrain. In the recruiting of horsemen, Xenophon clearly emphasises that physical endurance is as important as possession of wealth, and makes the sensible suggestion that preparation for service in the cavalry should begin while a youth was still under the control of his legal guardian, that is to say, before the age of eighteen (*Hipparchikos* 1.9, 11).

Marble bust (Paris, musée du Louvre) of Ptolemy. Made satrap of Egypt, he declared himself king only in 304 BC. After the downfall of Demetrios, he was joined by Demetrios' fleet, which enabled him to control the Aegean. He alone of his contemporaries died in his bed. (Fields-Carré Collection)

So far as we know, citizens in nearly all Greek city-states were organised by tribes (i.e. real or mythical kin groups), and it was on the basis of tribal affiliation that their citizen militias were mobilised. We certainly know that the citizens of democratic Athens were organised into ten tribes, and each of these furnished a tribe (*phyle*) of horse, each with a nominal strength of a hundred horsemen and headed by a tribal leader (*phylarchos*). The ten *phylai* of horse were under the overall command of two cavalry commanders (*hipparchoi*), each of whom would command in battle a wing made up of five *phylai*. All these equestrian officers would be elected annually, the two *hipparchoi* from the whole citizen body and one *phylarchoi* from each tribe. Presumably the horsemen of Taras were formed into similar tribal contingents, though we do not know how many.

As military service was continuous there was probably, as at Athens, an annual enrolment whose object was to fill the places of those who retired through old age or other causes. If this was the case, and it seems likely, every recruit had to appear with his mount, which, along with the equipment necessary for mounted service, he provided himself, before a board of (elected) magistrates responsible for the cavalry arm. Each recruit and his

Alexander Sarcophagus (Istanbul, Arkeoloji Müzesi, 370 T), Royal Necropolis Sidon, Alexander at Granikos (334 BC). Carried off eleven years later at the very height of his manhood vigour, like his ancestor and model Achilles, his able and ambitious generals soon strove with each other for supremacy. (Fields-Carré Collection)

PREVIOUS SPREAD: ENROLLING FOR CAVALRY SERVICE

Preparation for cavalry service began while a boy was still under the control of his legal guardian (usually his father), in other words before the age of eighteen. So our young horseman here would have mastered the difficult art of riding at an early age. On coming of age, however, his name had been added to an official register to constitute proof of his citizenship. As a citizen he was now liable for military service. For the juvenile-turned-adult, being an aristocrat, this meant performing his military service on horseback rather than on foot.

On a specific day of the year the aspiring cavalryman would have made his way to the agora of Taras and assembled along with other recruits before the magistrates responsible for the cavalry corps. The new recruits were now summoned before the magistrates, who then judged their fitness for service, mount included. In this scene we see a group of young men, dressed in *chamydes* and *petasoi* and carrying two javelins apiece, escorting their stallions towards two magistrates, one standing and one seated. The seated man, who wears a long *chitôn* under his draped mantle (*himation*) and is bearded, jots something down on a writing tablet, held in his left hand.

Meantime another magistrate, inspects a recruit's horse. In the opening chapter of the *Peri Hippikes*, Xenophon immediately makes himself useful by giving his reader "directions how best to avoid being cheated in buying a horse" (1.1). True to his word, Xenophon then proceeds to describe the various parts of the horse, starting at the hoofs and working methodically upwards to the head. The critical gaze and probing hand of the magistrate here tells us that he is both an excellent judge of a horse and a highly accomplished horseman. The young owner, undoubtedly anxious, holds the reins of his mount.

horse would be scrutinised for fitness for service. If passed, the recruits' names would be entered on the cavalry register. At the same muster, existing horsemen and their horses would also be scrutinised. As the names of those who requested release from the service on the basis of age or bodily incapacity would now be deleted from the register, this part of the enrolment was doubtless performed first.

The recruitment process was different for Tarentine mercenaries. By and large two types of mercenary recruiting were (and indeed still are) common. It was either carried out by recruiting officers or directly through diplomatic channels and inter-state treaties that included clauses allowing citizens to serve as soldiers for an agreed wage for the contracting parties. The latter was a tried and tested method as a state or ruler that needed mercenaries would procure them through a friendly power that controlled a source of supply. This was certainly the case during the great war between Athens and Sparta, with the latter state having some considerable influence over the traffic of mercenaries from the Peloponnese and, as a consequence, the friends and allies of the Spartans profited by being able to engage Peloponnesian mercenaries when necessary (e.g. Thucydides 3.109.2, 7.19.4).

When recruiting was not backed by diplomacy, the usual practice was to despatch or hire recruiting officers (*xenológoi*) to localities from which mercenaries were to be found or raised. Thus, the Spartans granted the recruiting officers of Dionysios, tyrant of Syracuse, permission "to enlist (*xenologeîn*) as many mercenaries from them" (Diodoros 14.44.2). Likewise, when the philosopher zealot Dion set out to liberate his native Syracuse from tyranny, he secretly collected a small mercenary army "through the agency of others" (*exenológei*, Plutarch *Dion* 22.3). Again, Eumenes, in response to the mounting threat from his enemy Antigonos, "selected the most able of his friends, gave them ample funds, and sent them out to engage mercenaries" (Diodoros 18.61.4). Plainly such men needed an intimate knowledge of the current mercenary market and, as such, doubtless included the entrepreneurial

Funerary painting from Paestum (Andriuolo Tomb 58, *c.* 350 BC). This Lucanian horseman bears a shield with a bronze rim and central grip. He wears a crested Attic helmet, bronze circular breastplate on cross-straps, and greaves. He is armed with a stabbing spear and *kopis*. (Fields-Carré Collection)

mercenary leader whose first responsibility was to negotiate the contract with the employer and then recruit and lead the men to fulfil it.

Finally, there were the casual methods of recruiting mercenaries. The most obvious of these methods was that of winning over mercenaries currently in the pay of the enemy. A true mercenary is a professional soldier whose behaviour is dictated not by his membership of a socio-political community, but his desire for personal gain. In short, his sole motivation is financial gain, and as such the mercenary does not discriminate between causes or states to which he offers his services.

Desertion and surrender on the part of the mercenaries were symptoms most common in the generation of the Successors, when the rapid rise and fall of the great employers was a hindrance to personal loyalty among soldiers, and an excuse for their keeping a weather-eye to the main chance. Thus the desertion of the troops of Perdikkas to Ptolemy, of Antigonos to Ptolemy, of Lysimachos to Antigonos, of Kassandros to Demetrios, or the wholesale surrender by the mercenaries of Krateros, occurred at various key engagements.

An attempt should now be made to tie all this in with our Tarentines. As we know some 2,300 Tarentines signed up with Antigonos for his war against Eumenes and, whatever their origin, they made a permanent place for themselves in the Antigonid army, since they were still with Demetrios at Gaza in 312 BC and at Athens in 307 BC. Thus, it appears that the Tarentines stayed loyal to the Antigonids even after the major reverse at Gaza when other Antigonid mercenaries decided to throw their lot in with the two victors, Ptolemy and Seleukos. Interestingly Diodoros recorded that the Tarentines had been recruited for "their loyalty", but a crashing defeat such as Demetrios experienced at Gaza would have pressed such fidelity to the breaking point.

History does not record the actual recruiting process for these particular Tarentines but we can confidently assume that they were hired by a recruiting officer on behalf of Antigonos. The main recruiting point throughout the region was Tainaron (present-day Cape Matapan). It was the southern-most tip of Lakonia and Greece, the ideal location from which to sail to Magna Graecia, Sicily, Crete, North Africa, Anatolia and the Near East. We can reasonably assume that Tarentines would have travelled to this point to join the Antigonid army.

EQUIPMENT AND APPEARANCE

It is possible, by the end of the third century BC if not much earlier, that the term Tarentine may have denoted a style of fighting or a type of horseman rather than a nationality, much like the use of Macedonian, and by this point in time largely only referred to weaponry and tactics. Unfortunately, our ancient authorities only hint at what this style of fighting may possibly be. From Diodoros, in his description of Antigonos's left wing at Paraitakene, we know that the Tarentines were adept ambushers. Not usually a martial skill suitable for the battlefield, but Diodoros does make the general point that on this wing Antigonos had posted "the lightest of his horsemen, who, drawn up in open order, were to avoid a frontal action but to maintain a battle of wheeling tactics" (19.29.1).

Livy, describing the last war between Philopoimen and Nabis, says the Tarentines were ordered to take up the van of the Achaian army, each man "leading two horses" (35.28.8) as they did so. Philopoimen, himself a horseman *par excellence*, then led the Tarentines into action, seizing a cliff overlooking a stream from which the Achaian army was to draw water. Livy also emphasises the rough and uneven nature of the terrain. The following morning, when a scuffle broke out on the banks of the aforementioned stream, Livy describes how the Tarentines employed by both sides came to blows, the skirmish for a time hanging in the balance because the opponents were "of the same character and fought with similar equipment" (35.29.3).

It appears, therefore, that the Tarentine style thus popularised was that of horsemen skirmishing with javelins. As for the two horses per man, well, the initial reaction to this piece of information is one of bemused scepticism. Diodoros does mention "two-horse men" (*amphippoi*, 19.29.2) at Paraitakene, and it can be argued that each of these brought an extra mount to battle. On the other hand, two horses per man on campaign would have been extremely difficult to maintain let alone expensive. Much later the Huns would make a practice of travelling with a number of reserve mounts to ensure that they always had a fresh one when needed (Ammianus 17.12.3), but on the Eurasian steppes horses were plentiful and horsemanship a matter of habit. It is possible to assume that the Tarentine version of the *amphippoi* could be another element of ceremonial equestrian games.

Finally, the works of the Greek historian Arrian describe lightly armed horsemen, what he called "pure Tarentines", who merely engage in shooting with javelins from afar or while riding in circles, and others, "light Tarentines", who are each armed with one javelin for shooting and a sword for close-quarter work (*Ars Tactica* 4.5–6, cf. Asklepiodotos 1.3). By his reckoning, therefore, there are proper Tarentines who engage the enemy by just shooting at him and imitation Tarentines who fight hand-to-hand with the enemy after having shot at him. It seems likely that Arrian's two types of Tarentines reflect a change over time in their tactical usage, namely from being the true skirmishers of our period to light-armed horsemen who could close with the foe if necessary.

Commissioned in AD 136 on the direct instructions of the philhellenic emperor Hadrian, himself a noted hunter and horseman, Arrian wrote the *Ars Tactica* (*Téchne Takitké* in Arrian's Greek), while serving as the governor of the frontier province of Cappadocia (AD 131–137). Throughout his work the author demonstrates a keen interest in older fighting formations, which is no less so with the equestrian section, and thus drew upon the Hellenistic manual tradition for inspiration. Naturally his main concern here is to postulate ways of adapting the infantry-based army of his own day to the new threats posed by the highly mobile horsemen from the steppe, the Alani.

Arrian may have drawn upon Asklepiodotos, the Hellenistic tactician, but it is Xenophon whom he had studied very closely before he worked on his *Ars Tactica*, even go so far as to adopt the *nom de plume* of Xenophon in this and his other technical works. Without a doubt the most valuable and instructive authority on Greek cavalry is the original Xenophon. Though his two equestrian treatises, *Art of Horsemanship* (*Peri Hippikes*) and *Cavalry Commander* (*Hipparchikos*), concern the horsemen of fourth-century Athens, Xenophon does provide us with excellent details about horses, riding, as well as the organisation and command of cavalry; in this respect his views are pertinent to the cavalry of other Greek city-states, including Taras.

Shields

It has been suggested that shield-bearing cavalry first appeared in the Greek world with the arrival of the Gauls in Greece (279 BC) and Anatolia (275 BC). Most historians agree that Gaulish horsemen carried shields with a central handgrip, controlling their mounts entirely by leg movements, but fourth-century coins of Taras already depict its horsemen using shields at a time when no other Greek horsemen did so. Indeed, Xenophon had recommended against it, and it is almost certain that the cavalrymen of Alexander did not carry shields.

Tarentine influence, it can be conjectured, was responsible for the spread of shields to other Greek horsemen. Greek horsemen probably adopted shields in the first quarter of the third century BC, either after the appearance of Tarentines in the army of Antigonos, or after Pyrrhos' Italian venture, when he had come face to face with the horsemen of Taras. On balance the second appears to be a more reasonable assumption rather than a rapid introduction after 317 BC. Dionysios of Halikarnassos says that Pyrrhos armed his royal bodyguard (*agêma*) with the Macedonian horseman's spear (*xyston*) in Magna Graecia, but after his return to Greece was himself using a bronze-faced shield on horseback in his last battle on the streets of Argos. Pausanias, the Greek traveller and geographer of the second century AD,

C | **EQUIPMENT FOR MERCENARY SERVICE**

As well as a round shield some of the horsemen are shown on Tarentine coinage carrying one or two javelins in the left hand, close to the horizontal. This suggests that the shield was held by a central handgrip held horizontally, as a double grip would lead to the javelins being held vertically. The shield itself was some 60cm in diameter, only slightly concave, and made of a thin bronze facing stretched over a light wooden core. One Period VII coin (Vlasto 789) shows a Tarentine horseman with a ribless shield blazoned with the popular eight-pointed star. He is also depicted wearing a *pilos* helmet adorned with a fore-and-aft horsehair crest (see page 59, bottom left).

This style of helmet derived from a felt conical cap actually called the *pilos*, which was first worn as a protection underneath helmets and later translated into bronze. The *pilos* helmet was light and gave all-round vision, and seems to have been adopted by the Spartans first. The helmet ends in a noticeable point, and has a narrow rim that does not stick out at all but follows the line of the crown, hanging almost vertically from the body of the helmet (see horseman, plate D).

The Attic style of helmet evolved from the 'Chalcidian' helmet. With good ventilation, hearing and vision without sacrificing too much facial protection, this had been a very popular helmet in its original form, especially in Magna Graecia and Sicily. However, improved versions with a cranial ridge for better protection and hinged cheek-pieces for better ventilation appeared. The nasal guard also became smaller and disappeared entirely from some helmets, giving rise to the Attic style in which the only vestige of the nasal piece was an inverted V over the brow. The horseman in the background of this plate wears an Attic helmet.

The horseman in the foreground wears a 'Thracian' helmet. It is distinguished by a small peak to protect the face from downward blows, while the skull is often high and curving like a cap. The cheek-pieces usually found with this style of helmet are more elongated than other types, closely shaped to the face and pointed at the chin.

As for the citizen cavalry, weapons are the standard choice of two or three cornel-wood javelins and a *kopis*. However, javelins, particularly those in the hands of professionals, could be equipped with the *ankyle*, a thin leather thong that was wound round the middle of the shaft to make a loop for the index and, usually, the second finger of the throwing hand. The loop provided leverage and acted like a sling to propel the javelin, and as it was launched the thong unwound, having the same effect as the rifling inside a rifle barrel: it spun the javelin, ensuring a steadier flight. The *ankyle* was never tied to the shaft of the javelin, but was merely wrapped round and came free after the throw. In the insert we see the method of holding a javelin by the *ankyle*, as used by a javelin-thrower. The first two fingers of his right hand have been inserted into this loop, while his two smallest fingers and thumb lightly grip the javelin shaft.

Seán Ó Brógáin '09

recorded that the Argives kept the shield as a trophy, displaying it at the entrance to the sanctuary of Demeter in their city (2.21.4), and what little remains of the bronze facing (and the honorific inscription) is now to be seen in the Archaeological Museum of Nauplion.

After having soldiered in Magna Graecia it seems likely that Pyrrhos re-equipped himself and those responsible for his personal protection when he fought on horseback, with shield and short spear or javelins. Pyrrhos was not just another heroic warrior running amok with a naked sword, for it must not be forgotten that he was a student of the science of warfare and had written a treatise on the subject.

Tarentine gold stater (Period III, Vlasto 434–5), young man leaping from his horse. In his left hand he holds a small shield, while with his right he clenches tight the reins of his cantering mount. This is probably a depiction of the *anabates*. (Fondazione E. Pomarici-Santomasi/Franco Taccogna)

The Tarentine coins also show small, round cavalry shields, approximately 45cm in diameter. This style may have evolved from the Italiote Greek equestrian event, the *anabates*, which was a race for horsemen carrying small shields, known from the fifth century BC onwards. Usually the horsemen are dismounting from a cantering horse, which appears to be an act of equestrian skill, other coins depict them being crowned with victory garlands. An ordinary horseback race, or *keles*, was usually run over six stades, that is, one run up and one down a hippodrome, approximately 1,200m. On the other hand, in the *anabates*, or dismounter, the rider dismounted for the last stretch and ran beside his horse. Its origins were military, since speed and agility were essential for a horseman in battle.

Polybios says Roman horsemen, before they adopted Greek arms and armour, were poorly equipped (6.25.3–7). Protection was a small ox-hide shield, which was too light for adequate defence at close quarters and tended to rot in the rain. Polybios actually compares its shape to a type of round-bossed cake, namely those that were commonly used in sacrifices; it may be the type shown in the Tarentine coins, with a flat rim and convex centre.

Body armour

Although Xenophon (*Peri Hippikes* 12.1–7) provides a comprehensive list of the essential body armour required by an aspiring horseman, sculptural and ceramic evidence suggest that horsemen disdained protection. The protective benefit of body armour could make a rider feel safer and more eager for combat, yet it was hot, heavy and cumbersome, and made manoeuvring on horseback extremely difficult, particularly without the aid of saddle or stirrups.

Muscled cuirass (London, British Museum, GR.1842.7.28.712), dated *c.* 320 BC. This is the front plate of bronze body armour for a horseman, as evident from the slight flaring at the waist. This helped him to bend at the waist and to sit on his horse. (Fields-Carré Collection)

A cuirass was not really suitable for a horseman since the extension over the abdomen made it awkward to bend at the waist and to sit on a horse. Similarly greaves were almost certainly impractical for horsemen, mainly because they would have interfered too much with the rider's grip. Before four-horned saddles, a Celtic innovation, much of a horseman's control was exerted through his legs, which needed to be able to grip the horse's flanks.

Helmets

In addition, crested Attic and *pilos* helmets are shown on some of the coins depicting the large shield, while others just depict the shielded riders bareheaded. It is interesting to note that the *pilos* helmet starts appearing on Tarentine coins not long after the Italian campaigns of Archidamos, and thus is probably worn as a result of Spartan influence.

This helmet type derived from a felt cap actually called the *pilos*. This simple, conical cap was quite possibly first worn as a protection underneath helmets, which was later translated into bronze. The *pilos* helmet was light and gave all-round vision, and seems to have been adopted by the Spartans first. The helmet ends in a noticeable point, and has a narrow rim that does not stick out at all but follows the line of the crown, hanging almost vertically from the body of the helmet.

As for the Attic style of helmet, it seems to have evolved from the Chalcidian helmet, so named after Chalcidian vases of the late sixth century BC, when it first appeared. These were actually manufactured in Magna Graecia, and southern Italy and Sicily have also produced about half the actual finds of Chalcidian helmets, which suggest it could have been invented there before coming to old Greece. With good ventilation, hearing and vision, without sacrificing too much facial protection, this had been a very popular helmet in its original form. However, improved versions with a cranial ridge for better protection and hinged cheek-pieces for better ventilation appeared later.

The nasal guard also became smaller and disappeared entirely from some helmets, giving rise to the Attic style in which the only vestige of the nasal piece was an inverted V over the brow. This type was extremely popular throughout the Italian peninsula. Crests, if worn, were most often white, red-brown or black, made from natural horsehair and could be dyed.

In addition, Attic helmets, adorned with crests, are also shown on some of the coins depicting small shields.

Attic helmet (Paris, musée de l'armée, E.4) from southern Italy, late fourth century BC.
The horse's head on the hinged cheek-piece suggests the helmet once belonged to a horseman. The Attic was less constricting than the earlier all-encompassing Corinthian. (Fields-Carré Collection)

Javelins

In the main, the group of coins that have survived to the present day depicting large shields also depicts the riders as being armed. The weapon itself is more than likely to be a javelin, especially so when a rider is shown to be carrying more than one weapon. In those cases when only a single weapon is depicted it is possible to claim that this is a short stabbing spear; however, considering the preponderance of javelin-armed riders here, the javelin appears to be the weapon *par excellence*. One javelin was used as a missile, the other either as a second missile or as a stabbing weapon, according to circumstances.

Swords

As a sidearm, horsemen normally used a recurved sword, the *kopis* (described as *falcata* in Latin). This had a heavy, one-edged blade designed for slashing with an overhand stroke. Both the cutting edge and the back were convex, weighing the weapon towards the tip. This was much favoured by Xenophon for cavalry use (*Peri Hippikes* 12.11), and several surviving examples – generally the longer ones – have horse head handles implying cavalry use. His preference was probably based on the fact that it was difficult for a horseman to stab with his sword and then extract it from the body of his victim. Thus, even from the unstable position atop a horse in close and crowded combat, the *kopis* was capable of delivering a murderous downward cut that could sever a victim's arm at the shoulder.

Horses

The Greek horse was a troublesome creature to ride, and given the conditions, although the cavalry was not always an efficient arm in the field, it is a mistake to suppose the individual Greek rider was a poor horseman. Their horses, familiar to us from the Parthenon frieze, were ungelded and unshod, they were prone to biting, and the rider had neither stirrups, nor saddle to assist him, while the curb bit, another Celtic innovation, was not to reach the Graeco-Roman world until the third century BC. When it did, it added to the normal or snaffle bit a chain or bar that fitted beneath the lower jaw in the chin groove. This gave the rider considerably more leverage.

As for size, the limited surviving osteological evidence indicates a range from 1.1 to 1.45m (10.3–14.1hh), with most being around 1.34m (13.1hh). A modern horse's height is measured just in front of the saddle, specifically at the withers, the unit of measurement being a hand of four inches (10.16cm). A horse of around 13.1 hands is some 2.1 hands smaller than the average cavalry charger in the early part of the 20th century. A good comparison in terms of horse size, workload, climate, and to some extent topography, would be with the small horse or the mounted infantry pony on field service in India during World War I.

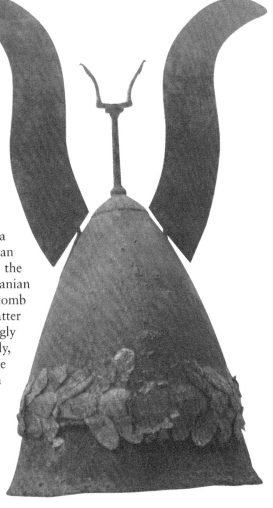

Pilos helmet (Paris, musée du Louvre, Bj.2152) from Italy, late fourth century BC. The decoration is Celtic but the style is Greek. Several helmets with wing-like attachments cut out of thin bronze sheet have been found in Apulia. (Fields-Carré Collection)

The Hungarian scholar Bökönyi has noted that the introduction of the blood of eastern horses, Scythian by Philip and Persian by Alexander, was to greatly improve the Greek horse. We know from the Roman epitomiser Justin that in 339 BC Philip defeated the Scythians and seized a considerable amount of booty, including 20,000 well-bred mares that were sent back to Macedon for breeding purposes (9.2).

As for specific breeds of Magna Graecia, Lucilius, a Roman satirist of the second century BC, says Campanian horses were fiery and mettlesome, though lacking the endurance of Iberian horses (frs. 506–8 Marx). Lucanian horses are not distinguishable from Campanian in tomb paintings, both being high-stepping and proud, but latter Roman writers call Lucanian steeds small-bodied and ugly in appearance and colour, though hard workers. Finally, Varro informs us that noted breeds are named from the districts from which they come, as "in Italy the Apulian from Apulia" (*de re rustica* 2.7.6).

As previously noted, a strong association of horse-breeding and wealth was evident in Greek social and political thought. Aristotle records the existence of a contemporary belief that the sons of kings ought to be educated in "riding and the art of war" (*Politics* 1277a18).

It is interesting to note that according to Xenophon some individuals lost money keeping horses, while others prospered through their sale (*Oikonomikos* 3.8–9). He records that he himself once sold a warhorse for fifty darics or 1,250 drachmae (*Anabasis* 7.8.6). Evidence from fourth-century Athens suggests the cost of a warhorse ranged from 100 to 700 drachmae, with most costing around 500 drachmae. Just to give you some idea of what this cost actually represents on a practical level, a manual labourer could guarantee to earn one drachma per day working on a civic building project in Athens (Fields 2003: 115).

Grooms

In his treatise *Peri Hippikes* (5.1–6.16) Xenophon advises the horseman on how to instruct his groom in stable management, grooming, leading and bridling the horse. Although these duties are to be carried out by a servant, the horseman is expected to keep a strict watch on his conduct. The emphasis is clear; a man who neglects his horse neglects his own safety. Xenophon in the *Hipparchikos* (5.6) has each man attended by a mounted groom in the Athenian cavalry corps, but these grooms did not ride in the ranks and were not armed.

A number of the Tarentine coins (Vlasto 510–15), all dated to *c.* 334–303 BC, bear the image of a working groom. Each is identical in that the groom is shown examining the uplifted left forefoot of the horse, crouching beneath the horse.

Funerary painting from Paestum (Andriuolo Tomb 61, *c.* 350 BC). This Lucanian horseman rides a dark chestnut with light-coloured mane and tail, white feet and face. Ancient horses had less prominent withers and backbone, and Greek and Italian breeds stood, on average, around 13.1 hands high. (Fields-Carré Collection)

Parthenon frieze (London, British Museum, west II). Horses are commonly shown without saddlecloths, but this could be artistic convention, the better to show the elegant lines of the horse's body. A simple woollen rectangle, the cloth was held on by broad breast strap and girth. (Fields-Carré Collection)

As already mentioned, horses were unshod, iron horseshoes having yet to be invented by the Celts, and mounts were apt to go lame, especially on rocky, dry terrain. Xenophon records that in one engagement he led his men on horseback until the ground became too difficult and he was forced to leave his horse behind (*Anabasis* 3.4.49). This, perhaps, explains his later recommendation to harden horses' hoofs by inducing them during grooming to stamp on a bed of round stones, each about the size of a fist (*Peri Hippikes* 4.4–5, *Hipparchikos* 1.16).

When the horse was led out to be groomed or given a roll, a muzzle was used so as to prevent the horse from biting without hampering his breathing (Xenophon *Peri Hippikes* 5.3). The muzzle is depicted on several Attic and south Italian red figure vases, and those for ordinary use were made either of straps or of wicker.

Weapons handling

Tarentine thus became a type of professional horseman equipped with several javelins and a large round shield, and fighting in a particular way, that is to say, useful for operations in difficult country, and for skirmishing movements in front of or apart from the main battle line.

In the *Hipparchikos* Xenophon advises that recruits, once they have acquired a firm seat, should be trained "to throw the javelin when mounted" (1.6). Obviously we would consider throwing the javelin on horseback a difficult feat since the Greek rider lacked stirrups, but the importance of this development has been over-emphasised by many historians, particularly in the military context. Stirrups are usually seen in terms of how they could help the horseman be more effective, especially when using weapons.

What is often overlooked is the fact that stirrups also gave support to the legs on long-distance rides. They also reduced the effects of the cold by improving the circulation in the rider's legs. This was, in truth, probably why they were developed in one of the coldest horse-rearing parts of the world, namely the Eurasian grassland belt. Of equal significance is the American scholar Gaebel's comment that with the stirrup it "became easier to ride with less skill, providing hitherto unknown lateral stability and making it easier to produce usable cavalry or dragoons in a comparatively short time from recruits with little or no experience with horse" (2002: 166 n. 29). As for

Greek horsemen, it was their natural skill and small mounts that allowed them to perform such acrobatics, not stirrups.

Undoubtedly an exceptional horseman himself, Xenophon provides the basic instructions for how to sit on a horse correctly:

> The lower leg including the foot must hang lax and easy from the knee down…The rider must also accustom himself to keeping the body above the hips as loose as possible, for thus he will be able to stand more fatigue and will be less liable to come off when he is pulled or pushed.
>
> *Peri Hippikes* 7.6–7

So Xenophon rejects the chair seat in favour of the straight leg seat. As the experienced equestrian Ann Hyland has recorded, this "position enabled the rider to move with his horse, feel the horse's back muscle movements and be forewarned of the horse's next move" (2003: 42). We should also remember that when attacking formed infantry Greek cavalry never charged home. On the contrary, they only approached near enough to launch their javelins with effect. In the *Peri Hippikes* Xenophon advises, for greater impetus and range, the rider to "advance his left side, draw back his right, rise from his thighs and let the javelin go with the point slightly raised" (12.13).

Naturally we have to assume that experienced bareback riders almost invariably have a better seat and more secure leg contact with the horse than would be possible with the security offered by stirrups and saddle. As well as being recommended by Xenophon, this poised style of riding is commonly depicted in the figured evidence.

Horses need daily exercise and riders, especially military ones, need practice, and this need for continued practice is emphasised again and again by Xenophon. To improve the rider's control over his mount, particularly in dangerous situations or in rough terrain, he recommends that training was to take place regularly and over all types of ground (*Peri Hippikes* 7.15).

However, equitation was as much an individual's responsibility as it was one for the state. The horseman should develop his own skills in riding, for Xenophon advises that when riding out to his country estate he should make

Greek *kopis* (Madrid, Museo Arqueológico Nacional), fourth century BC. This was a single-edged blade that widened towards the point. The thicker outer edge made it a strong slashing weapon. Used by foot and horse alike, with the equestrian ones being as long as 70cm. (Fields-Carré Collection)

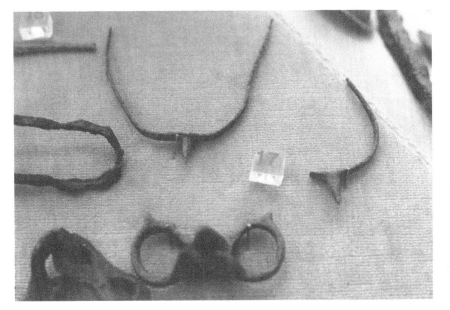

Bronze prick spurs (Paestum, Museo Archeologico). Normally with a short but sharp point, they were secured with thongs either to the bare heel or to the boot. Spurs were commonly made of bronze so as not to rust. (Fields-Carré Collection)

Lucanian red figure *pelike* (Policoro-Matera, Museo Archeologico Nazionale, 35304). Poseidon, 'Lord of horses' (Aristophanes *Knights* 551), on horseback accompanied by a young horseman (others reckon Athena). On the left rump of the horse appears a brand mark in the form of a caduceus. (Fields-Carré Collection)

D HORSE AND HARNESS

(1) Both Greek and Italian horses were lightly built, being around or 13.1 hands high, with small heads and fine legs. Most, if not all, warhorses were stallions, or so the artistic evidence implies. They were not shod. In Homer the traditional hue for horses was *xanthós*, the colour of fair human hair, in horses perhaps dun but more likely a light chestnut. By our period, however, red-bays, greys and blacks are also mentioned in the written sources. Similarly, the horses in contemporary art are mostly dark chestnuts with light-coloured manes and tails, less often blacks, in either case having white legs, feet and faces. Alexander's famous Boukephalas was black with a white blaze on his forehead, while a Frentani cavalry commander who attacked Pyrrhos at Herakleia rode a black steed with white feet.

(2) Xenophon mentions a man may ride bareback, but assumes saddlecloths are standard, at least for war. The cloth here is a simple rectangle – its chief function being to keep the horse's sweat from the rider's legs – and it is held on by broad breast strap and girth. A second cloth is worn over the first, and this acts as a thick saddle-pad. Xenophon actually prescribes a thick quilted saddlecloth "to give the rider a safer seat and not to gall the horse's back" (*Peri Hippikes* 12.9), and pads may derive from this. A saddlecloth may help to prevent sores on the horse's back too, but it did not add much to the rider's stability since it is apt to slip. Xenophon rebukes the Persians "for putting more coverlets on their horses than on their beds, for they think of sitting softly rather than securely" (*Kyropaideia* 8.8.19).

(3) A horse was controlled with bridle, reins and bit. The first bridle is of dark brown leather with bronze fittings (3a). The second example is of red leather, again with bronze fittings (3b). Sometimes a bridle could be in the Persian-style, that is to say, of linked bronze plates, as in the third example (3c). Reins generally match the leather of the bridle and they should, as Xenophon advises, "be of equal strength, not weak nor slippery nor thick, in order that the spear may be held in the same hand when necessary" (*Peri Hippikes* 7.9).

(4) Xenophon likewise recommends a 'flexible' in preference to a 'stiff' bit. As shown here (4a), the snaffle bit consists of two axles joined in the middle by two broad links, one link within the other. Next to the links are discs; then on either side a cheek-piece covered with four rows of sharp teeth. The cheek-pieces are to prevent the bit from sliding sideways in the horse's mouth, while the teeth, which press inward against either cheek, influence the horse's lateral movement. Next to the cheek-pieces come the branches to be attached to the bridle, and outside of these the branches of the reins. Discs, cheek-pieces and branches move on the axles. From each of the central links hangs a little chain, of three or four rings, in order, as Xenophon explains, "that the horse may feel after them with his tongue and teeth and not think of taking the bit against the jaws" (*Peri Hippikes* 10.9). The second example shown here (4b) represents a much simpler version of a 'flexible' bit, whilst the third (4c) illustrates a 'stiff' bit. Snaffle bits could be of iron, as in the first example, or of bronze, as in the second and third examples.

1

2

3a

3b

3c

4a

4b

4c

the most of the opportunities offered him for training himself and his horse. He should not stay quietly on the roads, but practise "galloping over all sorts of ground" (*Hipparchikos* 1.18). Xenophon also recommended the following regarding weapons handling practice:

It is a good method of training for two riders to work together thus: one flies on his horse over all kinds of ground and retreats, reversing his spear so that it points backwards, while the other pursues, having buttons on his javelins and holding his spear in the same position, and when he gets within javelin shot, tries to hit the fugitive with the blunted weapons, and if he gets near enough to use his spear, strike his captive with it.

Peri Hippikes 8.10

Obviously the blunt weapons allowed for realistic but risk-free training, but one of the best methods of training cavalry and improving their skills was by public displays and tournaments. As noted, later on in Hellenistic Athens there were equestrian games involving horsemen known as Tarentines.

Slab (London, British Museum, GR.1816.6–10.158) from the Athena Nike temple, Persian horseman (*c.* 425 BC). Superb horsemen, Persians would ride along the front of the opposition discharging volleys of arrows or javelins, then wheel away only to shoot at their foe as they retreated. (Fields-Carré Collection)

In the passage quoted above Xenophon seems to assume that the horseman is equipped with javelin (*akóntion*) and spear (*doru*), the former for throwing and the latter for stabbing. In fact this spear is possibly what he later calls the *doratos kamakinou*, a weapon he argues against because "it is both weak and awkward to manage" (*Peri Hippikes* 12.12), hence his advice to replace it by two Persian javelins of cornel wood. Indeed, for our shielded Tarentines the javelin would have been a more effective and flexible weapon. In its role as a stabbing weapon, either the over- or underhand grip was suitable against both mounted and dismounted opponents. In the case of the overhand grip, thrusting blows were aimed at the opponent's head and upper body, seeking the vulnerable face and neck, while the underhand grip was suitable for thrusts aimed at the soft underbelly and groin.

LIFE ON CAMPAIGN

At no point did Taras possess a standing army and all military service was part-time. The core of its military forces was a citizen militia, mainly composed of farmers. Citizens could not afford to spend much time away from their families and farms, and in particular were available for military service only during the slack agricultural period between the grain harvest in May and the vintage in September. A citizen militia could not be kept together continuously. It is easy to generalise about decadence and a decline in civic virtue, but the story of Taras (as told by the ancient sources) leaves the modern reader in no doubt that these were contributory causes of its eclipse. The Tarentines of the fifth century BC had regarded a summer's campaign as no more than part of their civic duty; the Tarentines of Pyrrhos' day were happy to resign that part of their civic duty to others. The exception, of course, were those who chose to offer their services to the wider world as Tarentine mercenaries.

Pay and conditions

The Athenian orator and statesman Demosthenes, drawing up plans for a standing army to face Philip II of Macedon, believed he could actually find mercenaries willing to serve Athens for as little as two Attic obols a day (4.20). Some accounts allude to the fourth century BC being the period of the 'four obol recruit'.

First, according to the eyewitness account of Xenophon (*Hellenika*, 5.2.21), in 383 BC Sparta made it possible for member-states of the Peloponnesian League, which it controlled, to contribute money instead of troops, at the rate of three Aiginetan (four Attic) obols per hoplite and four times that amount for a horseman. It is important to note that Xenophon calls the four obols, *misthós*, wages. In other words, the Spartans clearly intended to hire mercenaries at four obols a day to take the place of their allies. This was the same sum as had been estimated for the cost of a citizen-hoplite forty years before as recorded by Thucydides (5.47.6). The second

Grave stele (Thebes, Archaeological Museum) bearing low relief of a Macedonian cavalryman. He wears a Boiotian helmet and bronze or linen corselet, and is armed with a *xyston* and *kopis*. Such horsemen were not showy youths, but independent tough scions of the Macedonian nobility. (Fields-Carré Collection)

piece of evidence conveniently belongs to the closing years of the fourth century BC. A surviving fragment from Menander's lost comedy, *Olynthia*, refers to a soldier "serving with Aristotle and receiving the wage of four obols a day" (fr. 357 Kock). But specialist cavalry forces could expect a higher wage as noted above.

Alexander had been able to pay his Macedonian soldiers the equivalent of six Attic obols per day (Harding 102), and an indication of the low level generally of standard mercenaries' wages is provided by a comparison with the three Attic obols a day, which were being paid at this time according to the building accounts of Eleusis for 329/8 BC, to an unskilled slave labourer for his food (*IG* 2² 1672). Or again, exactly four Attic obols were being paid to the Athenian *ephebes* as a daily ration allowance (Anon. *Athenaiôn politeia* 42.3).

However, it is necessary to attempt to evaluate the buying power of four obols. To keep the argument simple we shall assume that the only expense the man really needed to meet out of this wage was that of his daily victuals, which, as we shall see below, he was expected to provide for himself.

Herodotos, in his account of Xerxes' invasion of Greece, reckons the Persian troops were receiving a daily ration of one *choinix* (one imperial quart or 1.087 litres) of cereal per man (7.187.2). It was the

Roman practice in the second century BC, according to the contemporary testimony of Polybios (6.39.13), to issue a monthly ration of cereal equal to two-thirds of an Attic *medimnos* to each legionary, which is more or less equivalent to the daily allowance of one *choinix* Xerxes' campaigning soldiers were receiving by Herodotos' reckoning. In a similar vein, Aristophanes suggests "for one giant loaf, use just one *choinix*" (*Lysistrata* 1207). All in all, the evidence allows us to assume that the basic daily diet of a soldier in our period would have consisted of one *choinix* of cereal, more or less.

In the early fourth century BC the everyday cost of grain in the Athenian agora, according to Aristophanes (*Ekklesiazusae* 547–8), was three drachmae per *medimnos*, which works out at 0.375 obols per *choinix*. Towards the end of the century the Athenian price for grain, according to Demosthenes (34.39), had risen to five drachmae per *medimnos*, which works out at 0.625 obols per *choinix*.

Both the classicists Parke (1933: 323) and Griffith (1984: 308) take two obols a day as the existence-minimum in the days of Philip, that is

Attic stele (Athens, National Museum of Archaeology, 2744), Athenian cavalryman in battle (*c*. 390 BC). Bareback riders have deeper seats with lower centres of gravity. They also have better control by virtue of the close contact between their thighs and flanks of their horse. (Fields-Carré Collection)

Marble statue (Athens, Acropolis Museum, 700) of horseman (*c.* 500 BC). Ancient horses were smaller and narrower, thus making it easier for riders to support themselves with their thighs. Thus, as Xenophon advises, the straight leg seat is much preferred to the chair seat. (Fields-Carré Collection)

to say, the bare minimum upon which a man could reasonably expect to keep himself alive.

As we have seen, the purchasing power of the military wage fell as the century progressed, yet it did not slump to a level that meant a mercenary's very existence was in jeopardy, assuming, of course, his pay had not fallen in arrears or had not been paid at all, an all too common experience for most soldiers in the hire of others.

By the latter half of the third century BC the standard rate of pay varied greatly over time and place, but generally it now included rations plus money in wages, though the former could be commuted in kind for cash. Wages were normally reckoned from the first of each month and paid at the end of that month, while rations were evaluated at one *choinix* of cereal per day. Contracts of employment were usually for nine or ten months but as mercenary pay was a heavy drain on the treasuries of Hellenistic states arrears were frequent.

Unfortunately our ancient authorities are somewhat vague when it comes to the question of whether or not mercenary cavalry, such as our Tarentines, were paid extra to feed their mounts. We do know that in times of war the citizen-troopers of Athens, who were not paid a regular wage, were given

Hand-mills (Selçuk, Arkeoloji Müzesi). Portable rotary querns such as these allowed soldiers to carry ungrounded grain and thus reduce the risk of spoilage. Easy to use, grain is grounded by the action of one grit stone being rotated over the other by means of a handle. (Fields-Carré Collection)

a stipend of one drachma per day for fodder as various sources attest to this. This suggests that the two drachmae paid per day to a hired cavalryman, which Xenophon mentioned above in connection with the Sparta system of substitution, was meant to cover both wages and fodder.

Of course war might bring death, disease, or a dearth of pay, but there was always the hope of a windfall. When Alexander finally reached Babylon, for example, he was able to distribute bonuses to his army, and this largesse included a bonus of two months' pay for the mercenaries of the original expeditionary force (Diodoros 17.64.6). Alternatively there was always the off-chance of securing a lucrative bounty such as the two *minae* (200 drachmae) promised by Ptolemy to each mercenary deserting Antigonos (Diodoros 20.75.1).

In all probability, however, the quickest road to wealth for the mercenary was by plunder, especially after victory upon the field of battle. After the victory of Ptolemy at Gaza, Diodoros says his army took from Coele-Syria to Egypt "what of the booty it was possible to drive or carry" (19.93.7). Again, in reference to Demetrios' Macedonian campaign against his rival Kassandros in 302 BC, Diodoros says "Demetrios was followed by 1,500 horsemen, no less than 8,000 Macedonian foot-soldiers, mercenaries to the number of 15,000, 25,000 from the cities throughout Greece, and at least 8,000 of the light-armed troops and of the freebooters of all sorts such as gather where there is fighting and plundering" (20.110.4). It was certainly through looting that mercenaries, our Tarentines included, made up any shortfalls in their wages.

Feeding the man
How to feed and water the men (and their animals) was probably the most important initial requirement on campaign, and one which found its way down to the humblest command. It was a constant in every military plan, and remains so to this day.

One cereal or another has formed the staple basis of the human diet in every corner of the world since agriculture first began. In the ancient Mediterranean world barley and wheat were the two main grains – oats were viewed as a weed and thus considered fit only for animals, while rye, the closest relative of wheat, was considered a 'northern' grain and was not consumed. Barley, unlike wheat, is normally husked and cannot be freed from its cover-glumes by ordinary threshing and is, therefore, roasted or parched prior to use. Unfortunately, this process destroys the gluten content of the grain – this determines the baking qualities of flour – thereby making it unsuitable for leavened bread. Still, as yeast was still unknown, 'bread' in the period of the Tarentine horsemen was really unleavened crust and would have looked somewhat like modern pita.

Barley was generally known as "fodder for slaves" (Athenaios 304b) and considered far less nourishing than wheat, so much so that by the fourth century BC the preference for wheat and the bread made from it, in wealthy circles at least, had ousted barley from its prominent position in the Mediterranean diet. Thus, wheat became the staple cereal of Greece, as in other parts of the Mediterranean basin, and barley the cheaper but less popular alternative.

Barley-meal was barley grain that had been milled, and soldiers (or their servants if they could afford to maintain one) had to convert their daily ration of grain into flour themselves. Thus hand-mills were to be found amongst the mundane equipment necessary for an army simply because they were, as Xenophon explains, "the least heavy amongst implements used for grinding grain" (*Kyropaideia* 6.2.31). This meant that the troops could carry unground grain and thus reduce the risk of spoilage, as well as allowing them to take advantage of grain collected on the march. Most soldiers, if not all, were accustomed to seeing the daily supply of grain being ground out by hand on the stone quern at home.

Arcadian shepherdess, Kanboti Valley, Kandila, a sight that is as common today as it would have been in the ancient world. The ancient Greek diet was unquestionably cereal based, with meat and fish eaten only as a relish. Sheep (and goats) were far more important as living providers of milk and cheese, and, of course, wool. Campaigning soldiers commonly ate bread and cheese. (Fields-Carré Collection)

PREVIOUS PAGE: HORSEMEN PLAYING THE 'TROY GAME'

Xenophon describes an Athenian equestrian civic event known as the *anthippasia*. It is a sham cavalry battle (*Hipparchikos* 3.11-13). Two sides, each made up of five tribal contingents, faced each other with one taking on the role of pursuers while the other flees. Presumably the two sides then switched roles and the manoeuvre is thus repeated. The side that operated best was judged victorious.

This scene is based on a fragment of a double-sided marble relief set up by one such victorious tribe. Dated to the early fourth century BC, this fine artistic representation gives us some idea of the event. A serried rank of prancing horses awaits the signal to charge. The tribal commander (*phylarchos*), who rides at the outer end of the line, is mature – he is heavily bearded – while the fresh-faced youths astride the other horses are keen to display their newly developed skills. They wear knee-length tunics and are bare-headed and bare-footed. Each of the riders carries a single javelin, the officer in addition has a *kopis*. He also wears calf-length boots and a *pilos* helmet.

Xenophon, however, recommends that the *anthippasia* be a more practical training exercise. When a trumpet sounds the two sides ought to charge one another at the gallop and ride through each other's lines. This manoeuvre should be repeated three times, successive charges being conducted at a quicker pace. Xenophon, as a seasoned horse-warrior, visualises his modified *anthippasia* not only offering a more spectacular display but also the best way of training horsemen to battle efficiency without the ultimate peril of a real enemy.

It is possible that we have a Roman parallel for Xenophon's ideas. For the Romans the so-called Troy Game (*lusus Troiae*) was an 'ancient' pageant revived by Caesar and supposedly derived from Troy, Rome's parent city. Virgil (*Aeneid* 5.545-602) obligingly traces this game back to Aeneas' funeral games for his dead father. It was a sham fight performed by two mounted troops of boys, one younger, the other older, and all drawn from the scions of noble houses in Rome. On a given command the two sides would advance on each other with spears at the level and, much like Xenophon's modified version of the *anthippasia*, charge and turn and charge again.

It was patently a dangerous game for the young participants, a tumble from a horse commonly resulting in broken limbs. The celebrated Greek physician Galen was only too familiar with the consequences of hard riding, which included injuries to the chest, the kidneys and reproductive organs, "to say nothing of the missteps of the horses, because of which riders have often been pitched from their seat and instantly killed" (*Exhortation for Medicine* 101).

On campaign, barley would be roasted and milled by a soldier using his barley grain. Then the soldier would take his flour and knead it with a little oil and wine, using a square of sheepskin as a kneading-trough, to produce a simple form of bread. The fresh dough was rolled into wafer-thin strips then baked quickly. The soldier would usually do this by twisting a strip around a stick and baking it over the hot ashes of his camp-fire.

Despite Xenophon's claim (*Kyropaideia* 1.2.11) that when he was truly famished even barley-bread tasted sweet, it was usually helped down with a little local wine and a wedge of cheese, with onions, garlic, olives and anchovies as likely accompaniments. These daily rations would quickly grow tiresome for campaigning troops. Aristophanes' chorus of citizen-soldiers rejoice at the return of peace, which brought with it freedom from helmet, cheese and onions (*Peace* 1126–9). These rations were commonly carried in a knapsack "that only smells of onions, vinegar and bad breath" (*Peace* 528–9).

On active service a soldier, mercenary or citizen normally served as his own quartermaster: "report with three days' rations", Aristophanes records (e.g. *Peace* 311), as the standing order in Athens, for example. If a campaign dragged on it may have been impossible to provide a regular supply of rations for the soldiers to purchase, either from markets organised by vendors travelling with them or from local markets discovered on the way, so they were expected to forage for their food, making full use of local resources.

The customary ancient Greek diet consisted of pulses, cereals, cheese, olive and fruit; fish and meat were rare, and if eaten they were done so as a relish. It must not be forgotten that to most ancient Greeks the lack of meat in their diet was an acceptable fact of daily life, but a shortage of grain was a great hardship. Recent research has put forward the following estimates for the diet throughout the ancient Greek world: 65–70 percent cereals; 20–25 percent fruits, pulses and vegetables; 5–15 percent oils, meat and wine.

Campaigning soldiers were glad to be given meat when it was a supplement to the barley ration, not a substitute for it. Thus they would survive on a basic ration of barley or wheat, while sharp, pungent, salty foods, such as dried fish or meat, which kept well, were to be carried as appetisers or relishes.

Feeding the horse

Xenophon emphasises the importance of sufficient fodder for horses so that they would be able to perform as well as required, "since horses unfit for their work can neither overtake nor escape" (*Hipparchikos* 1.3). A horse in its natural habitat, living on grass, would eat most of the time. As a grazing animal the horse requires food in small amounts frequently, thus it is better to feed a stabled horse about three or four times a day rather than only once or twice. Grass alone, even when supplemented by hay in the winter months, is not sufficient for working horses since it will not keep them in hard condition. To achieve this extra food, usually hard fodder in the form of cereals must be given.

The quantity of fodder necessary to sustain each horse depends upon its size and amount of work it has to perform. The ratio of cereals to hay can be varied, provided the horse always receives adequate food-value to sustain the amount of work it is doing. Modern horses are generally fed more hay and less cereal when they are not working. When in work, on the other hand, horses require less roughage, so the quantities of hay can be reduced, but require more protein so the cereal ration is accordingly increased. Oats, barley and maize are the most commonly used modern cereals, but barley is fattening, and usually slightly less barley or maize is given compared to oats. Modern barley has approximately 11 percent protein, as do oats and maize, but varieties grown today differ very much from ancient ones and, in the main, have far less nutritional content than ancient strains. It must not be forgotten, moreover, that maize was completely alien to the ancient world.

As ancient grains would have given much better nutrition than the modern feedstuffs, a smaller quantity could be fed and still achieve good results. At the turn of the 20th century British army cavalry horses were given a daily forage ration of 5.4kg of hay, 4.5kg of oats and 3.6kg of straw, divided into three or four feeds. In addition, chaff was mixed with feeds, and bran mash, sometimes with linseed cake, was given once a week. However, the evidence for cereal rations issued to ancient warhorses is not abundant. Polybios (6.39.13), in his description of the military procedures of the middle Republic, indicates Roman cavalry mounts were fed on a ration that was about 1.5kg dry weight of barley a day. In truth barley is not very suitable for horses as it is apt to induce short-windedness and sweating until digestive tolerance is achieved, but it is universal in recorded antiquity until the adoption of the northern fodder-grain oats in early medieval Europe.

In the bitter conflict between Sparta and the Achaian League, Tarentine horsemen could be found fighting on both sides. One such occasion was on the upland plain outside the Arcadian city of Mantineia (207 BC). The plain is seen here looking south-west from the Tourla Ridge. (Fields-Carré Collection)

The hay and green fodder mentioned most often and favourably in ancient agricultural literature is what we know as lucerne or alfalfa. The Greeks called it *Medikê poía* (Latin *medica*) as it originated from the lush Median plain where the famed Nisaean horses were raised. Renowned for its large size, the Nisaean horse was paramount of all the breeds in the east. It is said that the Persians had brought the rich Median grass with them into Greece in 490 BC with Datis' invasion force (Pliny *Historia Naturalis* 18.144). Seeds probably came in with their cavalry's fodder, and this fine blue grass from the horse-studs back in Media then became a food-crop for horses throughout the region. Good grass hays have a protein content ranging from 7–10 percent, whereas lucerne cut at the optimum time has almost double that.

However, on campaign the conditions for cavalry mounts would change considerably. The animals would have to live off the land and rely on frequent foraging expeditions to provide their fodder. There would have been periods of plenty and even more periods of scarcity for cavalry mounts, when riders would have become anxious over their own horses' welfare and the baggage train would only have been able to provide at best a minimal amount of cereal.

Sleep

An army marches on its stomach. Nevertheless, an army also needs its sleep and our campaigning horseman, be he citizen or mercenary, was no exception. When available, tents – usually of hide – were used to house the troops in the field. On the other hand, Xenophon and Aristotle both imply that sleeping rough under the stars was the norm. We also hear from our literary sources of soldiers bedding down for the night on mattresses of straw, rushes or leaves. For a warmer and more comfortable night's sleep a soldier (or his attendant) could easily opt to carry a simple blanket-roll (*strômata*).

A Greek, and therefore also Tarentine, camp was a rather jerry-built affair, a mixture of tents, improvised bivouacs, and men huddled together sleeping in the open air. Life in camp was anarchic by modern military standards, with soldiers going to bed, rising, and breakfasting pretty much as they pleased. Xenophon describes such a camp scene – the young Xenophon himself was likely present at the time – involving the cavalry of Athens. Even with the enemy close at hand, some horsemen were still slumbering in their beds while their comrades were already taking up their battle stations and the grooms were up and about currying the horses (*Hellenika* 2.4.6).

BATTLE

Greek cavalry, such as the horsemen of Taras, could not ride down hoplites if the latter maintained their formation. But they were useful for flank or rear attacks and for protecting their own formations from similar enemy action. They were also effective against hoplites once their phalanx had been broken or in harassing them on the march and in cutting off stragglers. Cavalry could threaten the enemy's food supply by preventing foraging. Greek cavalry could also hold its own against lightly armed troops, and here we should include the locals Taras warred against. Further, its usefulness for reconnaissance, patrolling, picket duty and forming a cavalry screen for the main formations was recognised.

All this was to change with Philip and Alexander, practitioners of a new type of warfare that was much more total in its aims and methods. This approach called for a combined-arms force that could shatter the cohesion of the enemy, before totally destroying them in the pursuit – what the military strategist Clausewitz would later call the strategy of defeat. To this end, therefore, they employed large units of steady cavalry to deliver a decisive charge at a critical spot in the enemy's line while the solid phalanx formation of grim, professional foot-companions (*pezhetairoi*), each wielding a deadly twelve-cubit *sarissa* (5.4m pike), held them up. This tactical plan was conceptually straightforward and simple; the one providing resistance, the other causing a collapse that permitted penetration.

Indeed, the strength of Alexander's army of conquest lay in the cavalry, the core of which was the little group of Macedonian warlords who formed the king's companions (*hetairoi*). It was also articulated down into tactical units called *ilai*, which were recruited according to district. Put simply, the cavalry were not only efficiently commanded but fostered a strong sense of tribal identity too. As much psychologically as physically, the Macedonians took advantage of the inherent moral superiority of close combat over the comparative safety of fighting at a distance.

In wedge-shape formations Macedonian horsemen penetrated the enemy battle line. Such a formation allowed the cavalry to shift its axis of advance rapidly, and was therefore crucial when seeking and exploiting a gap in the enemy's line. The wedge was ideally suited to penetrate a narrow breach in the enemy's front and widen it. In this sense, their disciplined manoeuvring at speed added to their formidable power. Now the horseman really assumed a significant place in combat, rather than being employed as a skirmisher or mounted archer as was the case with contemporary Greek or Persian horsemen.

All Hellenistic armies maintained the basic order bequeathed to them by Alexander and his father, relying initially on their own forces and then increasingly on mercenaries such as the Tarentines. Yet given the expense of maintaining a cavalry force, particularly one trained to engage in brutal hand-to-hand fighting, the ratio between horse and foot constantly declined in the course of the period in the major Hellenistic armies. By default rather than design, therefore, the ratio fell from about one to five after Alexander to about one to eight by the end of the third century BC. For instance, at Ipsos, which was probably the largest and most decisive battle ever fought by the Successors, the total number of horse in the two armies, which numbered 155,000, was some 20,500 horse (Plutarch *Demetrios* 28.6). Moreover, steady cavalry changed its role from that of deciding the battle to one in which its main role was to defeat their counterparts and ensure the pike-armed phalanx could advance unmolested. So initially the basic goal of the commander remained the creation of a gap in the enemy's line, as at Paraitakene (317 BC), while later battles often dissolved into slogging matches between opposing phalanxes, as at Sellasia (222 BC) or Raphia (217 BC).

As sarissa-armed phalanxes tended to win battles by slowly grinding down the opposition, light-armed cavalry, such as the Tarentines, came into their own. The phalanx was basically designed to resist a frontal assault and protection from this direction was obviously good. The formation was therefore mainly vulnerable to attack from the flank or rear, and particularly on the unshielded right flank. Tarentines could be deployed as a flank guard for these larger, more valuable, formations. They could also be used more aggressively, that is to say, thrown out in front as a forward screen, probably to break up the enemy formation and take the edge off their fighting spirit before the main attack, and to provide an elastic defence. Thus at Gaza (312 BC), it fell to their lot to be detailed to form a forlorn hope on the left wing of Demetrios' army (Diodoros 19.82.2). At Mantineia (207 BC) too, Philopoimen was to post the Tarentines in his employ well in front of his main battle line (Plutarch *Philopoimen* 10.5).

The offensive use of cavalry against infantry was far less common than the defensive use. The military historian John Keegan rightly stresses that "a horse, in the normal course of events, will not gallop at an obstacle it cannot jump or see a way through, and it cannot jump or see a way through a solid

---

F | **BATTLE**

Horsemen, who were ineffective against steady troops who kept their formation, became formidable opponents when riding down fleeing footsloggers. Indeed, Tarentines were not armed or equipped for shock action, but were employed in a skirmishing role, used to scout and raid, drive off the opposition's light-armed horsemen and ride down his skirmishers.

At Gabiene, as we know, Antigonos' Tarentines eventually determined the issue by their seizure of the enemy's baggage train. Eumenes' phalanx, spearheaded by the invincible Silver-shields, had rolled up the opposition, but these hard-bitten old-timers, concerned with recovering their worldly possessions, entered into negotiations with Antigonos and treacherously handed Eumenes over to him in exchange.

Mercenaries were generally better trained than citizen troops, with consequently better tactical flexibility, more experience and less prone to panic. However, mercenaries could be difficult to control especially when faced with the prospect of easy gain. In this scene the Tarentines, at large amongst the enemy's baggage train, experience the bloody chase as they run down their victims with pitiless blood-lust that seems to overwhelm soldiers when they themselves are suddenly released from the danger of death.

Javelins spent, the horsemen have resorted to their secondary weapon, the *kopis*. Artistic evidence reveals that the *kopis* was characteristically used in an over-arm stroke, brought down from above the head or shoulder. In the Hippocratic corpus (*On Head Wounds* 11) it is recorded that wounds delivered from above, as would be the case of those inflicted from horseback upon those on foot, are worse than one inflicted from the same level. Among the butchered are women and children.

line of men... for the shock which cavalry seek to inflict is really moral, not physical in character" (1988: 83). In other words, cavalry cannot charge into an infantry formation and shatter it by brute force, but rather cause the formation to flinch before the point of contact is made. At Herakleia, Pyrrhos finished off the Romans with a cavalry attack when they wavered under the onslaught of his infantry and elephants (Plutarch *Pyrrhos* 17.3). A similar, but less bloody result was achieved by Seleukos at Ipsos. He exploited the absence of the enemy horse, which was still in hot pursuit of part of his army, by repeatedly sending his cavalry around Antigonos' phalanx and threatening to attack, until part of it deserted to him terminating both the battle and the life of Antigonos.

On the other hand, the greatest slaughter of a defeated enemy was achieved in the pursuit and, of course, cavalry came into its own during the vigorous and bloody chase of the vanquished. For this role Tarentines were ideally suited. Yet when armies are chiefly made up of mercenaries, be they state professionals or hired soldiery, the strategy of defeat is much too costly in men and money. Far cheaper for our Hellenistic warlord to back his opponent into a tight corner so that he becomes convinced that it is useless to continue the fight.

On a dry salt plain somewhere in the Gabiene district it was Antigonos' Tarentines that finally determined the issue by their capture of the enemy's baggage train and by producing treachery in Eumenes' army (Diodoros 19.43.8, Plutarch *Eumenes* 19.1). It is important to understand that by this point in time almost all the armies of this period are mercenary, in as much as they are no way citizen militias, and the resultant corporate spirit of camp-life exhibits itself strikingly in one material form. This is the soldier's laager, which now comes to represent all that he values in life. Shunning the practices of contemporary Greek and Persian armies, Philip had stopped the use of wagons and carts, severely reduced the number of servants, and forbidden wives and women to accompany the army (Frontinus *Strategemata* 4.1.6). However, under the warring Successors the baggage train included the soldiers' women, children and slaves, and also all the army's worldly possessions, sometimes the result of years of looting. Hence, it becomes of the first importance for a general to safeguard his soldiers' small portable home. Eumenes may have come away victorious, but the so-called 'Silver-shields' (*argyraspides*) agreed to hand over their general, a Greek among Macedonians, and join Antigonos in return for their property.

The veteran Silver-shields, 3,000 in number, had begun service under Philip (for every man of them is said to have been sixty and above in 316 BC) and were unparalleled in battle experience and prestige. At Gabiene the Silver-shields had delivered a violent frontal charge in close order, shattered the opposing part of Antigonos' phalanx, and wheeling right and keeping formation, as on a parade ground, took the rest of the line in the flank and put it to flight. But ironically, at the battle where the Silver-shields had their finest hour, the outcome was invariably altered by a small band of Tarentines. Taking advantage of a wall of swirling white dust to slip unseen behind the enemy lines, the Tarentines successfully captured the baggage train. As for Antigonos, he immediately took advantage of the situation and, with an enormous army of some 80,000 behind him and now with approximately 45,000 talents in his war chest, proclaimed himself Lord of Asia. Thus, Antigonos' Tarentine mercenaries changed the course of one of the most important battles of the Successor era.

MUSEUM COLLECTIONS

Historians and chroniclers were numerous throughout the centuries under discussion, although few of their works survive. Thus the lack of a continuous narrative is a problem for much of the period, particularly the early and mid-third century BC. A very large number of non-literary texts survive, and such sources – inscriptions, pottery and coins – give us an alternative perspective of the period. On the other hand, these sources raise their own problems of interpretation and require specialised skills in order to be properly evaluated as they cannot speak to us in their own voice, as Xenophon did.

But we can consider ourselves fortunate that so many figured representations of ancient Greek horsemanship survive, particularly for our purposes, by way of Tarentine coins and south Italian red figure vases. Though it is impossible to identify different breeds of ancient horses from such representations, they are an invaluable source of information for portrayals of riders, armour, weapons, tack and clothing. The following describes the key sources of evidence used in this study of Tarentine horsemen.

Pottery
In the iconography of contemporary red figure pottery, the warrior, who often appears mounted or with a horse, is represented in a series of standard settings: bidden farewell as he departs for war, in combat, in a funerary scene, or returning in triumph.

Apulian column-kratêr by the Maplewood Painter (Tampa, Museum of Art, 86.102, *c.* 350 BC)
A young horseman wearing a short tunic – decorated with a wave pattern around the neck, vertical dots and a panel of white – Oscan belt, and high laced boots. He carries a small round shield, decorated with a star device, and wears a 'Thracian' helmet topped with white horsehair crest and two tall

Greek *kopis* (Madrid, Museo Arqueológico Nacional), fourth or third century BC, from Almedinilla, Córdoba. Its handle, in the form of a horse's head, curves back to guard the knuckles. This splendid example is richly decorated with silver inlay; the missing insets would have been bone or ivory. (Fields-Carré Collection)

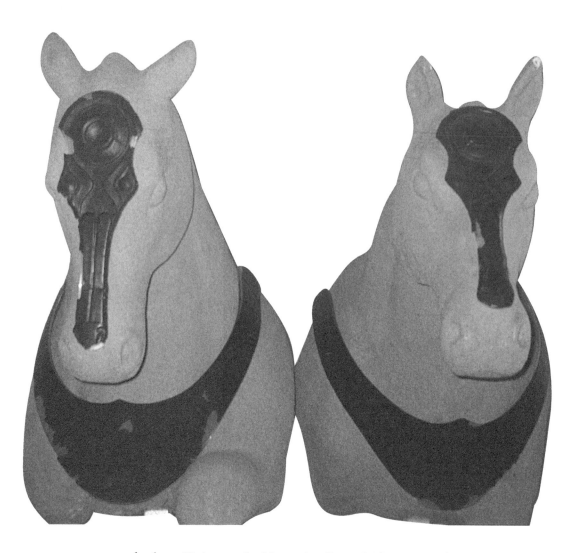

Fifth-century horse armour (Taranto, Museo Archeologico Nazionale, 73007–10) from Tomb 13.1.1935, Taras. At this period horse armour, if worn, was limited to a chamfron (face piece) and a poitrail (chest piece). These are of bronze plate that was once lined with linen or leather. (Fields-Carré Collection)

feathers. He is armed with two javelins, which are carried in the shield hand. There are white dots on the horse's bridle and chest strap, which may perhaps represent metal studs on the leather. As a point of interest, an Oscan belt was a broad leather belt covered in bronze sheeting, fastened with elaborate hooks and occasionally elaborately emobossed; it was the very symbol of masculinity.

Apulian volute-kratêr by the Baltimore Painter (John Paul Getty Museum, 77.AE.112, *c.* 340–330 BC)

A young horseman wearing a short red tunic stands beside a horse in a *naiskos*, a tomb in the form of a small temple destined to contain the statue of the deceased (a popular motif in Taras). The horseman holds a riding-whip in his right hand while his *pilos* helmet and sword hang from the rafters of the *naiskos*. He wears a Greek-style muscled cuirass, probably of bronze, and though depicted barefooted, he appears to be wearing Oscan bronze anklets.

Apulian *oinochoe* by the Patera Painter (London, British Museum, F.376, *c.* 330 BC)

A young horseman, wearing a patterned short tunic and Oscan belt, leans against his horse. A long spear is propped next to his left shoulder,

Xenophon's *doratos kamakinou*. He wears a wreath in his hair and boots that are low-laced with the upper end tucked into their tops. Above to his right hangs a pilos helmet, while beneath the horse lies a shield.

Apulian volute-kratêr by the Virginian Exhibition Painter (New York, private collection, *c.* 330–300 BC)

A young horseman, in a short red tunic and crested Attic helmet, stands beside a rearing horse in a *naiskos*. The horseman holds a long oval shield, reinforced with a bronze rim and a spine broadening to a spindle-shaped boss in the middle. This shield appears to be the Italic *scutum*, what the Greeks knew as a *thureos* or 'door-shaped'. His greaves are hung up on the rafters of the *naiskos*; horsemen rarely wear greaves, sometimes using Oscan bronze anklets instead.

Apulian volute-kratêr by the Baltimore Painter (London, British Museum, F.284, *c.* 325–320 BC)

A young nude horseman, wearing a red cloak, stands beside a horse in a *naiskos*. Propped against his left shoulder is a *doratos kamakinou*, and in his right hand he holds a wreath. A *pilos* helmet and Greek-style muscled cuirass of bronze hang from the rafters of the *naiskos* (see photograph on page 58).

Apulian volute-kratêr by the Baltimore Painter (LA County, Museum of Art, M.80.196.1, *c.* 320 BC)

A young horseman, wearing a short tunic and Oscan belt, stands with a horse in a *naiskos*. The horseman holds the bridle with his left hand. In his right he

Terracotta votive (Paris, musée du Louvre, MNB.1757) from Taras (c. 350–325 BC). This takes the form of a full-size *pilos* helmet with crest holder. Side A, the goddess of war and wisdom, Athena. Side B, the chief Amazon, Hippolyte. (Fields-Carré Collection)

Apulian red figure volute-kratêr (London, British Museum, F.284), dated *c.* 325–320 BC. Propped against the left shoulder of a young horseman is a *doratos kamakinou*, a weapon suitable for 'pig-sticking'. A *pilos* helmet and muscled cuirass hang from the rafters of the *naiskos*. (Fields-Carré Collection)

holds a spear that carries a butt-spike. From the rafters of the *naiskos* hangs a *pilos* helmet and sword.

Apulian volute-kratêr by the Arpi Painter (Tampa, Museum of Art, 87.36)

A horseman stands beside his horse in a *naiskos*. He wears a short tunic – highly decorated – under a linen corselet. He also wears a *pilos* helmet adorned with two feathers. He holds two javelins in his right hand and wears a prick spur on his left ankle.

Campanian *hydria*, Astarita Group (New York, Metropolitan Museum of Art, 01.8.12, *c.* 350–320 BC)

Greeted by a woman wearing full Oscan dress and attended by a servant in Greek dress, who holds a *phiale* and an *oinochoe*, a returning young horseman is depicted in a short tunic and Oscan belt. He also wears an Attic helmet with two tall feathers. He carries on his left shoulder a *tropaion* with large shield and streamer attached. The latter is almost certainly an Oscan belt, the spearhead having been thrust through the bronze sheeting. These represent spoils, often bloodstained, stripped from dead or captured enemy, a custom that goes back to Greek rule in Campania. Indeed, Frederiksen (1968: 15–24) suggests a Greek origin for the Campanian horsemen of the fourth century BC.

Campanian *hydria* by the LNO Painter (Budapest, T.763, *c.* 320 BC)

A woman in full Oscan dress, who is accompanied by a boy wearing a short tunic and Oscan belt, offers a *skyphos* of wine to a returning horseman. The horseman wears a short tunic, Oscan belt and Oscan triple-disc cuirass of bronze. He carries a large shield, decorated with what looks like a star device, and wears a 'Thracian' helmet adorned with two tall feathers and a white horsehair crest.

Campanian *skyphos* by the Libation Painter (Ruhr-Universität, Bochum Antiken Museen, S.996)

A woman in Oscan dress offers a *skyphos* of wine to a returning horseman. He wears a short tunic and Oscan belt. He also wears an Attic helmet decorated with three tall feathers. He carries on his left shoulder a *tropaion* with a large shield and streamer attached. The latter is almost certainly an Oscan belt.

Campanian calyx-kratêr, Horseman Group (Naples, Museo Archeologico Nazionale, 861/82599)

A combat scene shows a horseman attacking a Greek hoplite with a javelin; the latter begs for his life by raising both hands towards his assailant. The young horseman wears a short red tunic with a pattern of white three-dot rosettes and a white trim around neck and armholes. He also wears an Oscan belt and a *pilos* helmet with a horsehair crest and two feathers. He carries two extra javelins in his left hand and appears to be wearing high-laced boots.

Campanian calyx-kratêr, Horseman Group (Naples, Museo Archeologico Nazionale, 1985/82410)

A young horseman, wearing a wreath, stands beside his horse in a *naiskos*. He wears a short purple tunic and Oscan belt. He carries two javelins, which rest in the crook of his left arm. Above him to the right and hanging from the rafters

BELOW LEFT
Tarentine silver didrachma (Period VII, Vlasto 789–91), shield-bearing cavalryman. He wears a crested *pilos* helmet and has two javelins, held horizontally, in his shield hand. On his large shield is an eight-pointed star, a popular blazon in the period. (Fondazione E. Pomarici-Santomasi/Franco Taccogna)

BELOW RIGHT
Tarentine silver didrachma (Period VIII, Vlasto 877–81), with shield-bearing cavalryman. As well as the javelin in his right hand, which he is employing in a downward thrust, the horseman carries two more in his shield hand. (Fondazione E. Pomarici-Santomasi/Franco Taccogna)

of the *naiskos*, is a large round shield, very much like the *aspis* of a hoplite. On the left rump of the horse appears a brand mark in the shape of a circle.

Campanian squat *lekythos*, related to the Danaïd Painter (London, British Museum, F.242)

A horseman stands before an altar and alongside his horse holding its reins. He wears a short tunic, Oscan belt and triple-disc cuirass of bronze. He also wears an Attic helmet and in his left hand he holds a javelin. Beneath the horse lies a small round shield decorated with a circle of dots.

Campanian squat *lekythos*, Spotted Rock Group (Paris, Galerie François Antonovich)

Patting the muzzle of his horse, a horseman stands before an Ionic column. He wears a short tunic, Oscan belt and Oscan triple-disc cuirass of bronze. He also wears a *pilos* helmet and carries two javelins in his right hand. To the left of the Ionic column sits a woman who offers the horseman a *skyphos* of wine, while behind the latter stands another woman who carries an unrecognisable object in her arms.

Lucanian *pelike*, Karneia Group (Policoro-Matera, Museo Archeologico Nazionale, 35304, end of fifth century BC)

Poseidon, who served as protector of horses and patron of horsemanship, on horseback accompanied by a young horseman (others have suggested Athena instead) wearing a short tunic and Oscan belt. The horseman is unarmed but wears a crested Attic helmet. On the left rump of the horse appears a brand mark in the form of a caduceus (see photograph on page 38).

Lucanian Type II *nestoris* by the Choephoroi Painter (whereabouts now unknown)

Two horsemen are shown in combat with a single Greek hoplite. The horseman nearest, bareheaded and barefooted, wears a loincloth and Oscan belt. In his right hand is a spear with butt-spike. On the right rump of his horse appears a brand mark in the shape of a broken cross.

Lucanian bell-kratêr by the Anabates Painter (London, British Museum, 1978.6–15.1, *c.* 400–375 BC)

A naked youth, carrying a small round shield in his left hand, leaps from his cantering horse while retaining the bridle in his right hand. To his front stands a Nike, who offers him a victory wreath. Behind the horse is turn-post, a fluted column with an Ionic capital.

Category of coins as defined by M. P. Vlasto

Period	Date
II	430–380 BC
III	380–344 BC
IV	344–334 BC
V	334–302 BC
VI	302–281 BC
VII	281–272 BC
VIII	272–235 BC

continues on page 61

Coinage

The characteristic type of Tarentine coinage was a young male dolphin-rider, either Taras, son of Poseidon, after whom the city was named, or Phalanthos, the leader of the first settlers and about whom fanciful tales were later woven. For instance Pausanias says (10.13.10) that he was shipwrecked on his way from Greece and was carried to Italy on the back of a dolphin. Then came the long series of Tarentine coins called horsemen, of which the obverse type is a horse and rider, the horse galloping, cantering or standing still, the rider varying in age, attitudes and accoutrements. The coins themselves are categorised by period and number according to the collection formed by M.P. Vlasto. The examples illustrated in this book are on permanent display in the

Period	Vlasto
	Large shield
III	448
IV	522–4, 538–59
V	566–650
VI	691–6, 708
VII	710–31, 761, 789–802
VII	877–81, 890–903, 927–33
	Medium(?) shield
III	376–85, 443–7
IV	530–5
VI	679–82
	Small shield
II	297–315, 342–5
III	387–95, 428–42, 496–7
VII	683–90, 698–703
	Crested Attic helmet
II	297–300
III	376–85, 387–95, 443–8
IV	522–4, 530–5
V	589–98
VI	679–82, 698–700
VII	713–14, 716–31
VIII	890–903, 927–33
	Crested *pilos* helmet
V	648–50
VII	761, 789–802
	Bareheaded
II	301–15, 342–45
III	428–42, 496–7
IV	538–59
V	566–88, 599–647
VI	683–96, 708
VII	710–12, 715(?)
VIII	877–83

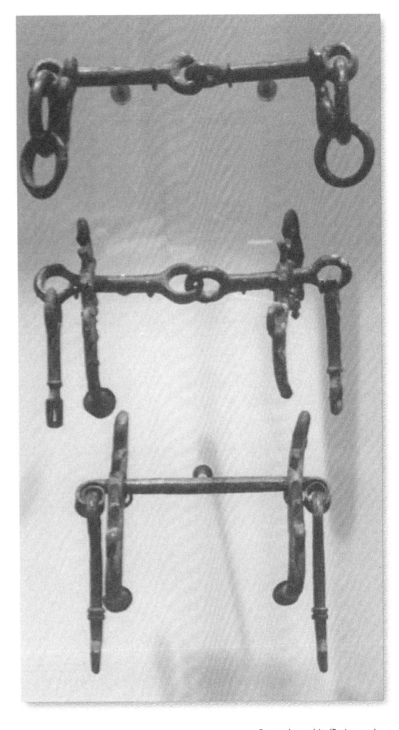

Javelin

One javelin, right hand	600–1, 890–3, 896, 898–900
One javelin, shield hand	297–8, 437–42, 443–7(?), 683
Two javelins, shield hand	387–8, 522–4, 648–50, 761, 789–99
Three javelins, two in shield hand and one in right	538–59, 566–7, 691–6, 708, 710–31, 877–83

Bronze horse bits (Paris, musée de l'armée, E.53–4, E.56a) from southern Italy. These are fourth-century snaffle bits; the top pair being what Xenophon calls 'flexible' types while the bottom one is the simple form, namely a single bar. (Fields-Carré Collection)

Museo della Fondazione Ettore Pomarici-Santomasi, Gravina in Puglia. I shall take the opportunity here to express my warmest thanks to the Fondazione for granting me the permission to use these photographs, which were shot and processed for me by my good Gravinese friend, Franco Taccogna. Other coins can be seen in Taranto (Museo Archeologico Nazionale), London (British Museum), and Glasgow (Hunterian Museum).

GLOSSARY

Akóntion	javelin
Choinix	dry measure equivalent of a man's daily grain ration (Attic *choinix* 1.087 litres)
Cubit	unit of measurement equal to the length from the elbow to the tip of the middle finger (Attic cubit 0.45m, Doric cubit 0.49m)
Drachma	standard weight as well as silver coin (Attic drachme = 6 obols)
Doru	spear, Greek horsemen using what was called a *doratos kamakinou*
Hoplite	heavily armed foot soldier accustomed to fighting shoulder-to-shoulder in a phalanx
Ila	tactical unit of horse
Kopis	single-edged, heavy slashing-type sword shaped like a machete
Medimnos	dry measure equal to 48 Attic *choinikes*
Mina	unit of weight equal to 100 Attic drachmae or 70 Aiginetan drachmae
Obol	smallest unit of weight and coinage (Attic-Euboic *obolos* 0.72g)
Sarissa	Macedonian pike
Talent	fixed weight of silver equivalent to 60 *minae* (Attic-Euboic *tálanton* 26.2kg, Aiginetan *tálanton* 43.6kg)
Xyston	Macedonian horseman's spear

Tarentine silver didrachma (Period VI, Vlasto 691), shield-bearing cavalryman and legend. From his cantering horse the rider thrusts downward with his javelin, while holding two in reserve in his shield hand. Javelins could be readily used both for throwing and thrusting. (Fondazione E. Pomarici-Santomasi/Franco Taccogna)

BIBLIOGRAPHY

Anderson, J.K., 1961. *Ancient Greek Horsemanship*. Berkeley: University of California Press

Bökönyi, S., 1974. *History of Domestic Mammals in Central and Eastern Europe*. Budapest: Akadémiai Kiadó

Brauer, G., 1986. *Taras: Its History and Coinage*. New York: Aristide D. Caratzas

Bugh, G.R., 1988. *The Horsemen of Athens*. Princeton: Princeton University Press

Connolly, P., 1981, 1988. *Greece and Rome at War*. London: Macdonald

Engels, D.W., 1978. *Alexander the Great and the Logistics of the Macedonian Army*. Berkeley: University of California Press

Everson, T., 2004. *Warfare in Ancient Greece: Arms and Armour from the Heroes of Homer to Alexander the Great*. Stroud: Sutton

Ewer, T.K., 1982. *Practical Animal Husbandry*. Bristol: John Wright & Sons

Fields, N., 2003. 'Dexileos of Thorikos: a brief life'. *Ancient History Bulletin 17*: 108–26

Frederiksen, M.W., 1968. 'Campanian cavalry: a question of origins'. *Dialoghi di Archeologia 2*: 331

Gaebel, R.E., 2002. *Cavalry Operations in the Ancient Greek World*. Norman: University of Oklahoma Press

Garouphalias, P., 1979. *Pyrrhus, King of Epirus*. London: Stacy International

Griffith, G.T., 1935, 1984. *The Mercenaries of the Hellenistic World*. Chicago: Ares

Hammond, N.G.L., 1989, 2001. *The Macedonian State: The Origins, Institutions and History*. Oxford: Clarendon Press

Harris, H.A., 1963. 'Greek javelin throwing'. *Greece & Rome 10*: 2636

Head, D., 1982. *Armies of the Macedonian and Punic Wars 359 BC to 146 BC*. Worthing: Wargames Research Group

Hyland, A., 1990. Equus: *The Horse in the Roman World*. London: Batsford

Hyland, A., 2003. *The Horse in the Ancient World*. Stroud: Sutton

Kraay, C.M. & Hirmer, M., 1976. *Greek Coins*. New York: Abrams

Keegan, J., 1976, 1983. *The Face of Battle: A Study of Agincourt, Waterloo and the Somme*. London: Barrie & Jenkins

Lomas, H.K., 1993. *Rome and the Western Greeks 350 BC – AD 200*. London: Routledge

Parke, H.W., 1933. *Greek Mercenary Soldiers: From the Earliest Times to the Battle of Ipsus*. Oxford: Clarendon Press

Rutter, N.K., 1997. *Greek Coinage of Southern Italy and Sicily*. London: Spink

Schneider-Herrman, G., 1996. *The Samnites of the Fourth Century BC: As Depicted on Campanian Vases and in other Sources*. London: Institute of Classical Studies

Scullard, H.H., 1974. *The Elephant in the Greek and Roman World*. London: Thames & Hudson

Sekunda, N.V., 1986, 1987. *The Ancient Greeks*. Osprey: Oxford (Elite 7)

Shipley, G., 2000. *The Greek World after Alexander, 323 – 30 BC*. London: Routledge

Snodgrass, A.M., 1965. *Early Greek Armour and Weapons*. Edinburgh: Edinburgh University Press

Spence, I.G., 1993, 2001. *The Cavalry of Classical Greece: A Social and Military History*. Oxford: Clarendon Press

Trendall, A.D., 1969. *The Red Figure Vases of Lucania, Campania and Sicily, 2 vols*. Oxford: Clarendon Press

Trendall, A.D., 1989. *Red Figure Vases of South Italy and Sicily*. London: Thames & Hudson

Ueda-Sarson, L., 2004. 'Tarentine cavalry'. *Slingshot 236*: 21–5

Worley, L.J., 1994. *Hippeis: The Cavalry of Ancient Greece*. Boulder, CO: Westview

Wuilleumier, P., 1939. *Tarente des origines à la conquête romaine*. Paris: De Boccard

Tarentine silver didrachma (Period V, Vlasto 589), shield-bearing cavalryman. Armed with three javelins and protected by a large round shield and an Attic helmet, this Tarentine horseman is suitably equipped for his various light roles as raider, skirmisher, flank-guarder, and pursuer. (Fondazione E. Pomarici-Santomasi/Franco Taccogna)

INDEX

References to illustrations are shown
in **bold**.